ELEMENTS

By John Favicchia

Edited by Joe Bergamini

Executive Producers: Dom Famularo and Joe Bergamini

Layout by Willie Rose and Joe Bergamini

Music Engraving by Ryan Carver, Willie Rose, and Stephane Chamberland

Solo Transcriptions by David Giacone

Additional solo transcriptions by Willie Rose

Cover Design by Michele Heusel

Cover Photo by Carolyn Wright-Chierico

CD Recorded by John Favicchia

Additional CD editing by Jimmy Wilgus

See page 6 for CD Credits

Alfred Item # 00-37007
ISBN: 0-7390-7618-3

www.wizdom-media.com
WIZDOM MEDIA PUBLICATIONS
PO Box 45, Whippany, NJ 07981 USA

John at Music Academy 2000, Bologna, Italy, 2009.

Mike Pope and John at Drum Fest 2005, Toms River, NJ.

Table of Contents

About the Author..4

Introduction..5

Key..5

About the Disc..6

PART 1: 16TH-NOTE ELEMENTS
1. 16th-Note Elements..8
2. Element Improvisations..15
3. Accented Element Rolls..22
4. 16th-Note Element Applications..28
5. Additional Applications..31
6. Ensemble Playing 1..32
7. Ensemble Playing 2..41

PART 2: 16TH-NOTE ELEMENT GROOVE OSTINATOS
1. 16th-Note Elements on the Bass Drum...................................51
2. 16th-Note Element Basic Groove Ostinatos............................52
3. 16th-Note Element Advanced Groove Ostinatos......................54

PART 3: TRIPLET ELEMENTS
1. 8th-Note Triplet Elements...59
2. Element Improvisations..64
3. Accented Triplet Element Rolls...66
4. Triplet Element Applications...70
5. Additional Applications..71
7. Triplet Ensemble Playing 1...72
8. Triplet Ensemble Playing 2...76

PART 4: TRIPLET ELEMENT GROOVE OSTINATOS
1. Triplet Elements on the Bass Drum.......................................81
2. Triplet Element Groove Ostinatos...82
3. Advanced Triplet Element Groove Ostinatos..........................83

PART 5: BASS PLAY-ALONGS..86

PART 6: PLAY-ALONG CHARTS
"Funk it Up"..91
"From Silence to Sound"..92
"Rock it Out"...93
"Coincidence"..94
"Te Estremeces"...96
"Animation"...99
"The Gauntelt"...102

PART 7: TRANSCRIPTIONS..106
"Introduction Solo"..107
"The Gauntlet" Solo...108
"World Time II" Solo..111
"Dharma" Solo...113
"Soloing With Elements 6 & 11"...115

John's Setup..117

Acknowledgements..118

About the Author

One of today's top players, New York-based John Favicchia has performed and/or recorded with such greats as Steve Khan, Tony Levin, Chieli Minucci, Lonnie Plaxico, John Benitez, Harvie S, Larry Coryell, Dean Brown, Rachel Z, Chris Geith, Laco Deczi, Mike Pope, John Benitez, Steve Adelson and Bob Malach. His band, Dharma All Stars, blends various styles into a powerful blast of fusion that spans the extremes of the dynamic range. Favicchia has been busy touring around the world as well as releasing his own albums. His debut CD, *World Time*, earned rave reviews and was a Top 10 Critics Pick of the Year in *Jazziz* magazine, while his latest release, *Dharma*, offers an intriguing mix of melody, eclecticism, and tight ensemble playing with a cast of all-star guests including Steve Khan, Dean Brown, Dave Mann, and Chieli Minucci. Favicchia enjoys both the mental and physical sides of playing drums. "Definitely," says John, "It's all about the soul and the mind, but its very visceral as well. I'm caressing the sounds out of my cymbals in one bar, but when the music takes off and I start to wail, I take no prisoners."

Increasingly in demand for drum clinics and festivals, John has recently performed at the following events:

John Favicchia/Bruno Farinelli Drum Clinic Tour - Italy 2009 & 2010
John Favicchia/Chris Lesso Drum Clinic Tour - Canada 2009 & 2010
John Favicchia/Mike Sorrentino Clinic Tour - United Kingdom & France 2010
John Favicchia Drum Clinic Tour - China 2010
Cape Breton International Drum Fest, Nova Scotia, Canada
Denver Music Institute, Denver, CO, USA
Drummers Collective NYC, USA
Quebec City Music, Quebec City, Quebec, Canada
Just Drums, Toronto, Ontario, Canada
Slam Jam Drum Festival 2005, NJ, USA
East Coast US Guitar Center Tour
Sam Ash Music US National Tour
Long Island Drum Center, Plainview, NY, USA

According to Mike Lomonaco at Just Drums in Toronto, "John Favicchia is great. He's a dynamic, very involved player who blew us all away with his great playing and personality."

John endorses Yamaha Drums, Sabian Cymbals, Vic Firth Sticks, Remo Drumheads, Latin Percussion, Hansenfutz Practice Pedals, Axis Pedals, DrumFun, Beatnik, Factory Metal Percussion, and Samson Mics.

You can contact John through any of the following resources:

E-mail: drummrfav@aol.com
www.johnfavicchia.com
www.youtube.com/drummernyc
www.facebook.com/johnfavicchia
www.myspace.com/johnfavicchia
www.twitter.com/johnfavicchia
www.linkedin.com/pub/john-favicchia/12/99/966

Introduction

Elements is a method for connecting your musical ideas with technique. It allows you to create and play an extensive vocabulary while thinking of basic rhythmic ideas. Basically, the Elements are simple one-beat permutations of eighth notes, sixteenth notes, or triplets (The Elements concept can work for any rhythm at all, but in this book we focus on eighths, sixteenths, and triplets, since these are the most frequently encountered rhythms in most music). The basic approach to this book is to learn these basic one-beat rhythms, and then practice them in specific ways on the drumset so that you can develop a vocabulary that will allow you to play any ensemble figure you might encounter, or solo around any given rhythm, and generally build a much more sophisticated vocabulary on the drums. If you practice and apply the Elements correctly, you will never get lost when playing fills, solos, and grooves.

Elements is also a way of thinking. If you think about all of your drumming as elements, you will be able to bridge the gap between all of your playing styles, solos, fills and grooves.

The Elements concept began because drum students were coming to me for lessons who had amazing hand and foot technique, but lacked the ability to completely utilize their technique skills on a full drumset. Their technique was at a very high level on a single surface (for example, on a pad or snare drum), but they were not applying all the knowledge they had on that one surface to the drumset.

el·e·ment
1. A fundamental, essential, or irreducible constituent of a composite entity.
2. The basic assumptions or principles of a subject.

per·mu·ta·tion
1. A complete change; a transformation.
2. The act of altering a given set of objects in a group.
3. Mathematics: A rearrangement of the elements of a set.

As you go through the book, you will learn the Elements and various ways to apply them on the drums, including using them for rolls and fills, playing enesemble figures, and soloing around hits.

Key

About the Disc

The enclosed disc is a data/MP3 disc. It will play on most newer CD players as a standard CD, or it can be loaded into your computer and imported into any music software such as iTunes.

1. Opening Solo & Introduction
2. 16th-Note Elements 1b
3. 16th-Note Element Improv 1
4. 16th-Note Element Improv 2
5. 16th-Note Element Improv 3
6. 16th-Note Element Improv 4
7. 16th-Note Element Improv 5
8. 16th-Note Element Rolls
9. 16th-Note Element Rolls Improv 1
10. 16th-Note Element Rolls Improv 2
11. 16th-Note Element Rolls Improv 3
12. 16th-Note Element Rolls Improv Full Set
13. 16th-Note Element # 11 One-Bar Fill
14. 16th-Note Element # 11 One-Bar Fill Voicings
15. 16th-Note Element # 11 Continuous Voicing Exercise
16. 16th-Note Element Hits On Beat 1 96bpm
17. 16th-Note Element Hits On Beat 1 130bpm
18. 16th-Note Element Hits On Beat 2 96bpm
19. 16th-Note Element Hits On Beat 2 130bpm
20. 16th-Note Element Hits On Beat 3 96bpm
21. 16th-Note Element Hits On Beat 3 130bpm
22. 16th-Note Element Hits On Beat 4 96bpm
23. 16th-Note Element Hits On Beat 4 130bpm
24. Bass Drum Elements Groove
25. Elements On Bass Drum: Song Example
26. Triplet Elements 1c
27. Triplet Elements Improv
28. Triplet Elements Improv Solo
29. Triplet Roll Elements Improv
30. Triplet Roll Elements Improv 3b
31. Triplet Element Hits On Beat 1 110bpm
32. Triplet Element Hits On Beat 1 132bpm
33. Triplet Element Hits On Beat 2 110bpm
34. Triplet Element Hits On Beat 2 132bpm
35. Triplet Element Hits On Beat 3 110bpm
36. Triplet Element Hits On Beat 3 132bpm
37. Triplet Element Hits On Beat 4 110bpm
38. Triplet Element Hits On Beat 4 132bpm
39. Bass Line – Rock Groove 1
40. Bass Line – Rock Groove 2
41. Bass Line – Rock Groove 3
42. Bass Line – Rock Groove 4
43. Bass Line –3/4 Funk
44. Bass Line – Blues 1
45. Bass Line – Blues 2
46. Bass Line - Jazz Trading 4 Slow
47. Bass Line - Jazz Trading 4 Medium
48. Bass Line - Jazz Trading 4 Fast
49. Bass Line - Jazz Trading 8 Slow
50. Bass Line - Jazz Trading 8 Medium
51. Bass Line - Jazz Trading 8 Fast
52. Bass Line - Jazz Trading 12 Slow
53. Bass Line - Jazz Trading 12 Medium
54. Bass Line - Jazz Trading 12 Fast
55. Bass Line - Jazz Trading 16 Slow
56. Bass Line - Jazz Trading 16 Medium
57. Bass Line - Jazz Trading 16 Fast
58. Bass Line - Salsa/Songo 118bpm
59. Bass Line - Salsa/Songo 135bpm
60. Bass Line - Samba 94bpm
61. Bass Line - Samba 120bpm
62. Bass Line - Partido Alto 90bpm
63. Bass Line - Partido Alto 102bpm
64. Bass Line - Bembe
65. Bass Line - Baiao 120bpm
66. Bass Line - Baiao 130bpm
67. "Funk It Up"
68. "From Silence To Sound"
69. "Rock It Out"
70. "Coincidence"
71. "Coincidence" No Drums
72. "Te Estremeces"
73. "Te Estremeces" No Drums
74. "Animation"
75. "Animation" No Drums
76. "The Gauntlet"
77. "The Gauntlet" No Drums
78. Opening Solo
79. "The Gauntlet" Drum Solo
80. "World Time ll" Solo
81. "Dharma" Solo
82. Element 6 & 11 Improv Solo

Audio examples played and recorded by John Favicchia

"Funk It Up" (Bill Heller/John Favicchia)
Bill Heller: Keyboards and programming

"From Silence to Sound" (Bill Heller/John Favicchia)
Bill Heller: Keyboards and programming

"Rock It Out" (Bill Heller/John Favicchia)
Bill Heller: Keyboards and programming

Bass line play-alongs performed by Mike Pope
Written by Mike Pope and John Favicchia

"Coincidence" (Chris Geith)
John Favicchia - Drums
David Mann - Tenor Sax
Chris Geith - Keys & Synth Programming

"Te Estremeces" (Mario Cazeneuve)
John Favicchia - Drums & Clave
Harvie Swartz - Vertical Bass
Mario Cazeneuve - Keys & Vocals
Mark Gatz - Soprano Sax & Tenor Sax
Carl Fischer - Trumpets
Ed Leone - Trombone
Cristian Riveria - Congas, Bells, Timbales
Matt Cardin - Nylon-String Guitar
Joe Torres - Vocals

"Dharma" (John Favicchia)
John Favicchia - Drums

"Animation" (Chieli Minucci)
John Favicchia - Drums
Chieli Minucci - Guitars & Synth Programming

"The Gauntlet" (Dean Brown)
John Favicchia - Drums
Dean Brown - Guitars & Keys
Jerry Brooks - Bass
David Mann - Tenor Sax

PART 1:
16th-NOTE ELEMENTS

"To reach a higher level, just when you think you are giving all you can give, that's the time to give more. Give 110%!"
- Dom Famularo

1. 16th-Note Elements

Here are the 16th note Elements. These are all the possible permutations of one beat of sixteenth notes. It is important to be 100% proficient in each one of these. These Elements will become the crucial building blocks of your drumming vocabulary. Practice these individually on a pad or snare drum, with a metronome, until they are comfortable.

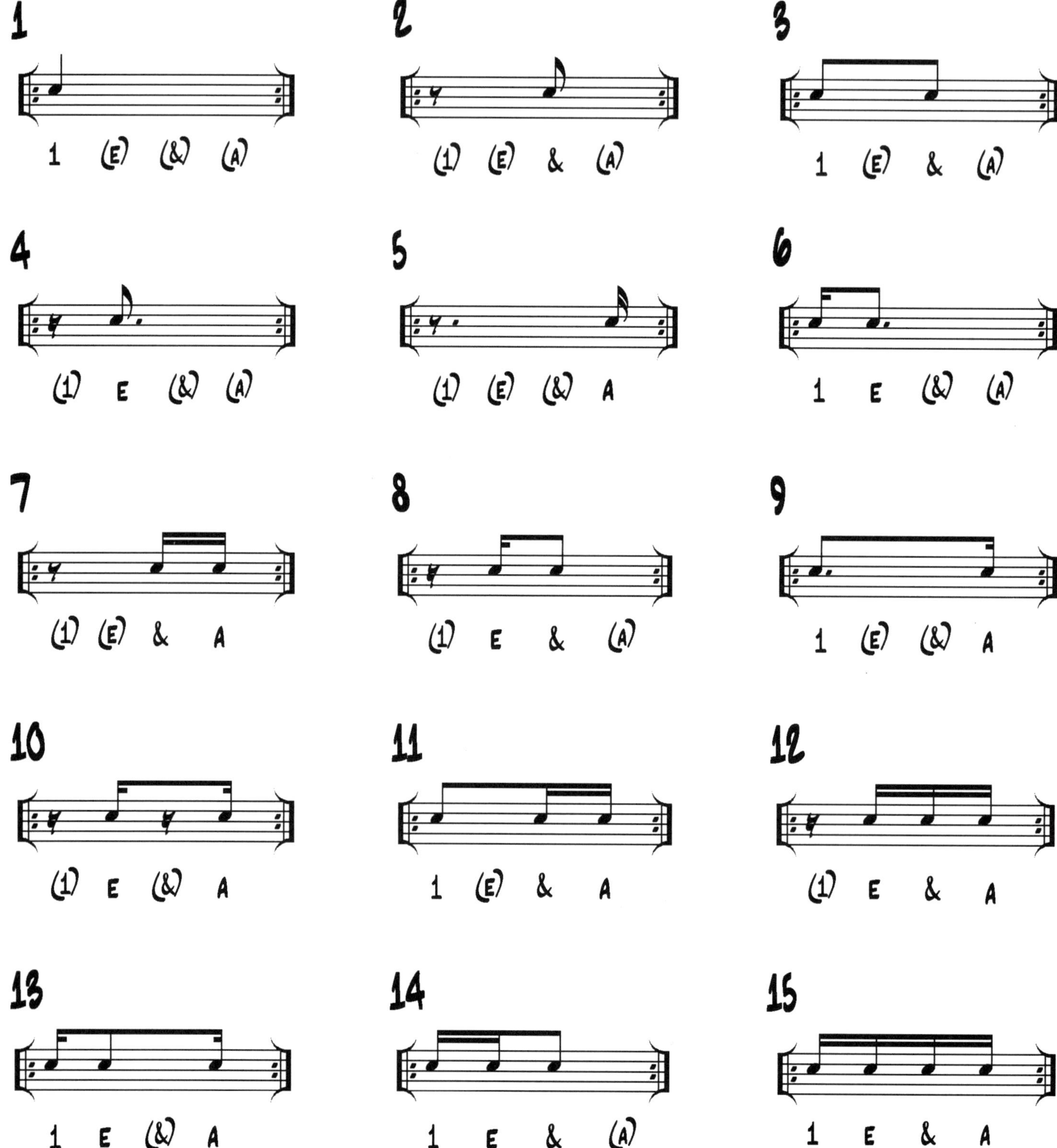

1a. Basic Elements Exercise

The following exercises are repetitions of each Element to make sure you are comfortable with them. Make sure to count the 16th-note subdivisions out loud. This is a time for you to break the Elements down and analyze them. This is just a practice drill; it doesn't yet have anything to do with applying the Elements with a band.

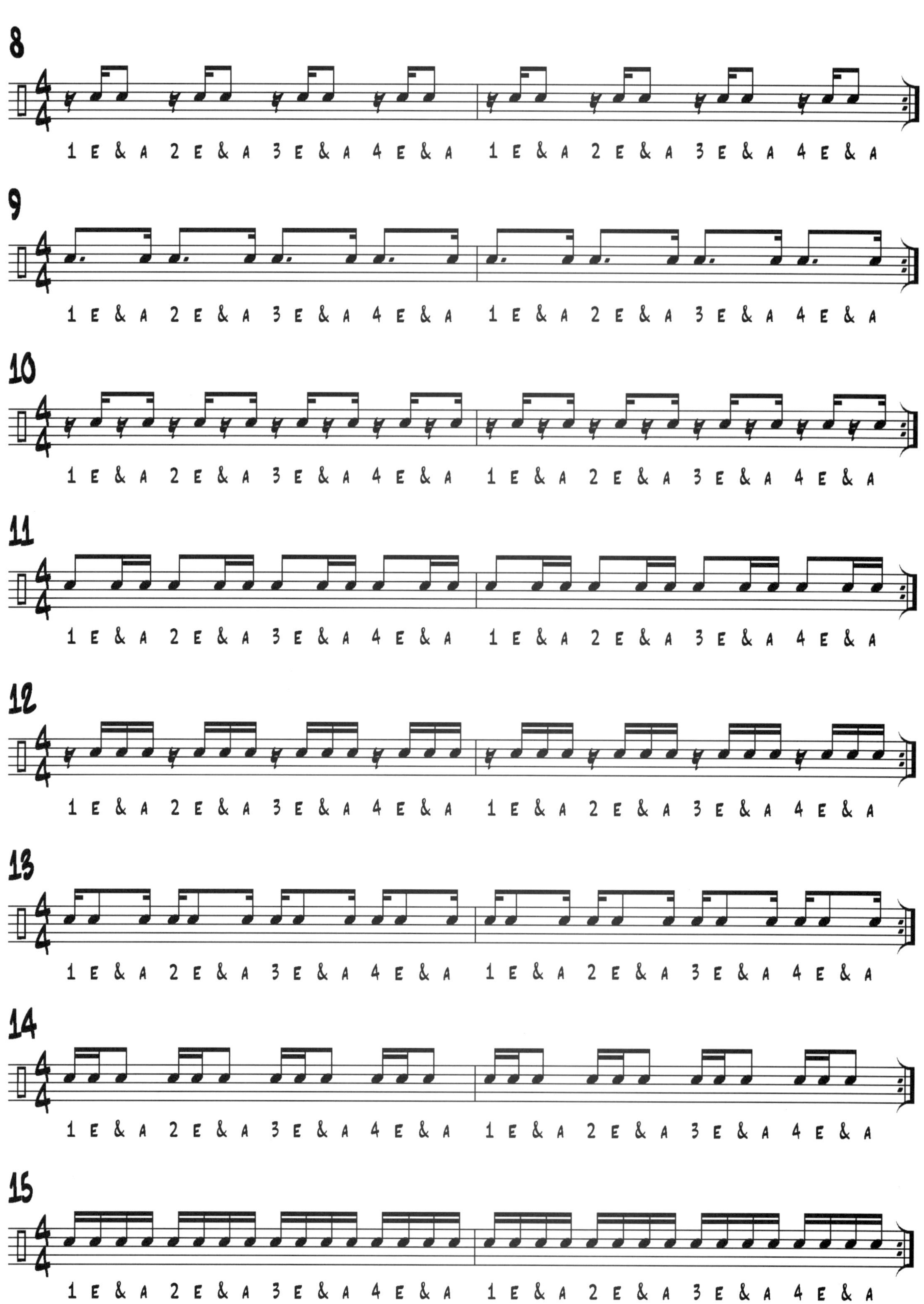
8
1 E & A 2 E & A 3 E & A 4 E & A   1 E & A 2 E & A 3 E & A 4 E & A
9
1 E & A 2 E & A 3 E & A 4 E & A   1 E & A 2 E & A 3 E & A 4 E & A
10
1 E & A 2 E & A 3 E & A 4 E & A   1 E & A 2 E & A 3 E & A 4 E & A
11
1 E & A 2 E & A 3 E & A 4 E & A   1 E & A 2 E & A 3 E & A 4 E & A
12
1 E & A 2 E & A 3 E & A 4 E & A   1 E & A 2 E & A 3 E & A 4 E & A
13
1 E & A 2 E & A 3 E & A 4 E & A   1 E & A 2 E & A 3 E & A 4 E & A
14
1 E & A 2 E & A 3 E & A 4 E & A   1 E & A 2 E & A 3 E & A 4 E & A
15
1 E & A 2 E & A 3 E & A 4 E & A   1 E & A 2 E & A 3 E & A 4 E & A

CD Track 2

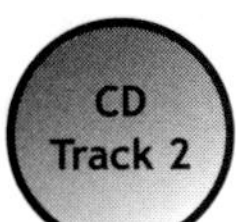

1b. Accented Elements

This exercise takes a steady flow of hand-to-hand sixteenth notes on one surface and adds the Elements to them in the form of accented strokes within the sixteenth-note flow. Play the 16th notes as low strokes (2-3" off the drum) and then accent the Elements as full strokes (9-12" off the drum). Dynamic control is key in this exercise; you must clearly execute the accented Elements at a clearly different volume than the non-accents.

1

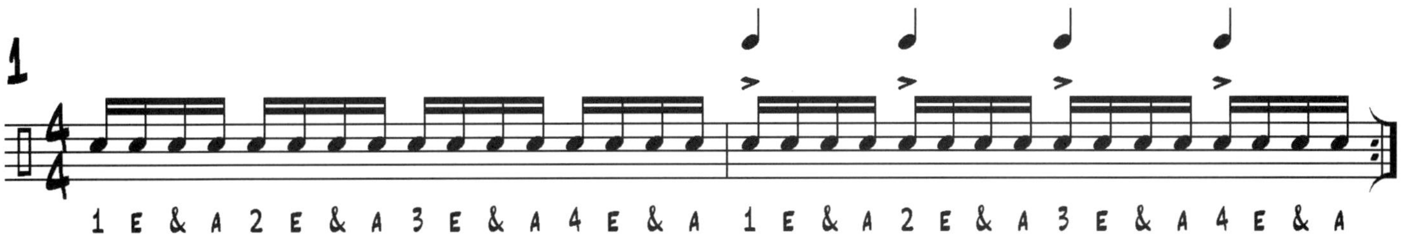

2

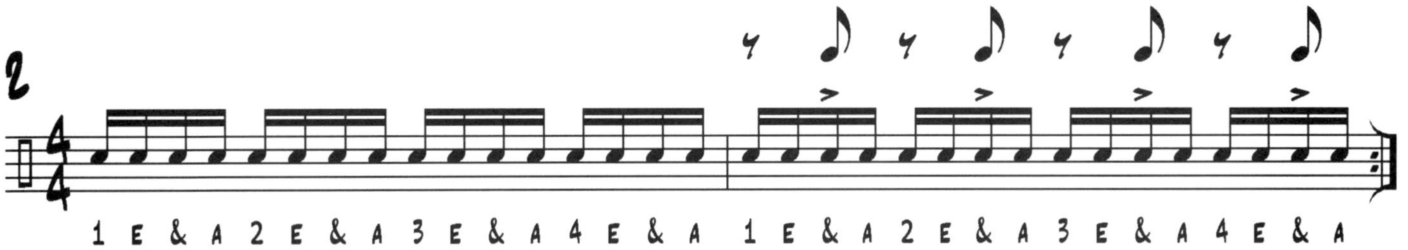

3

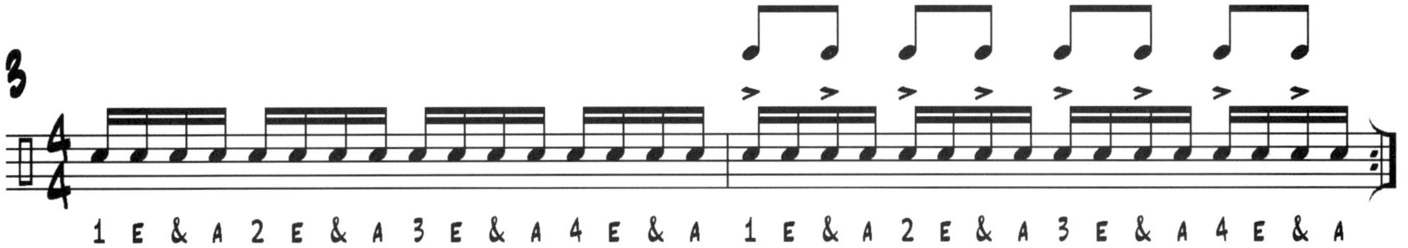

4

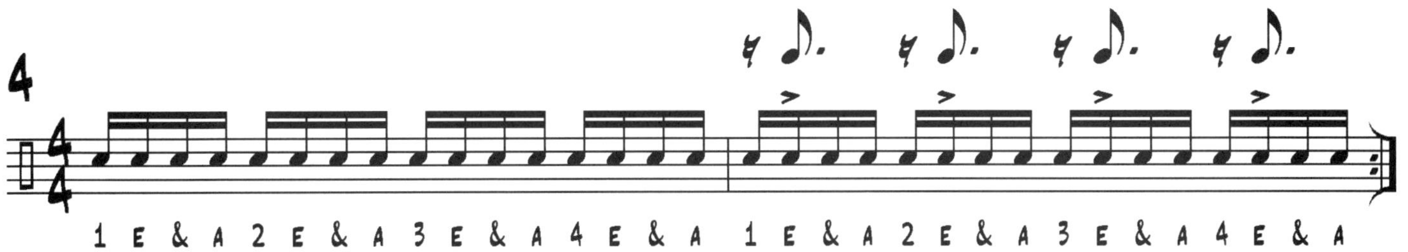

5

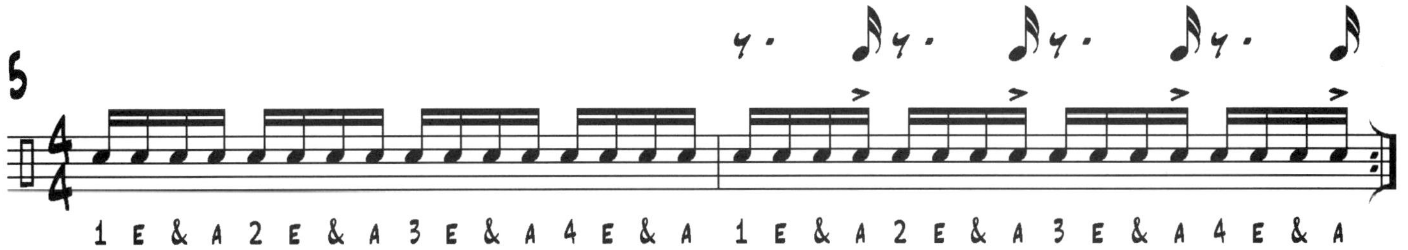

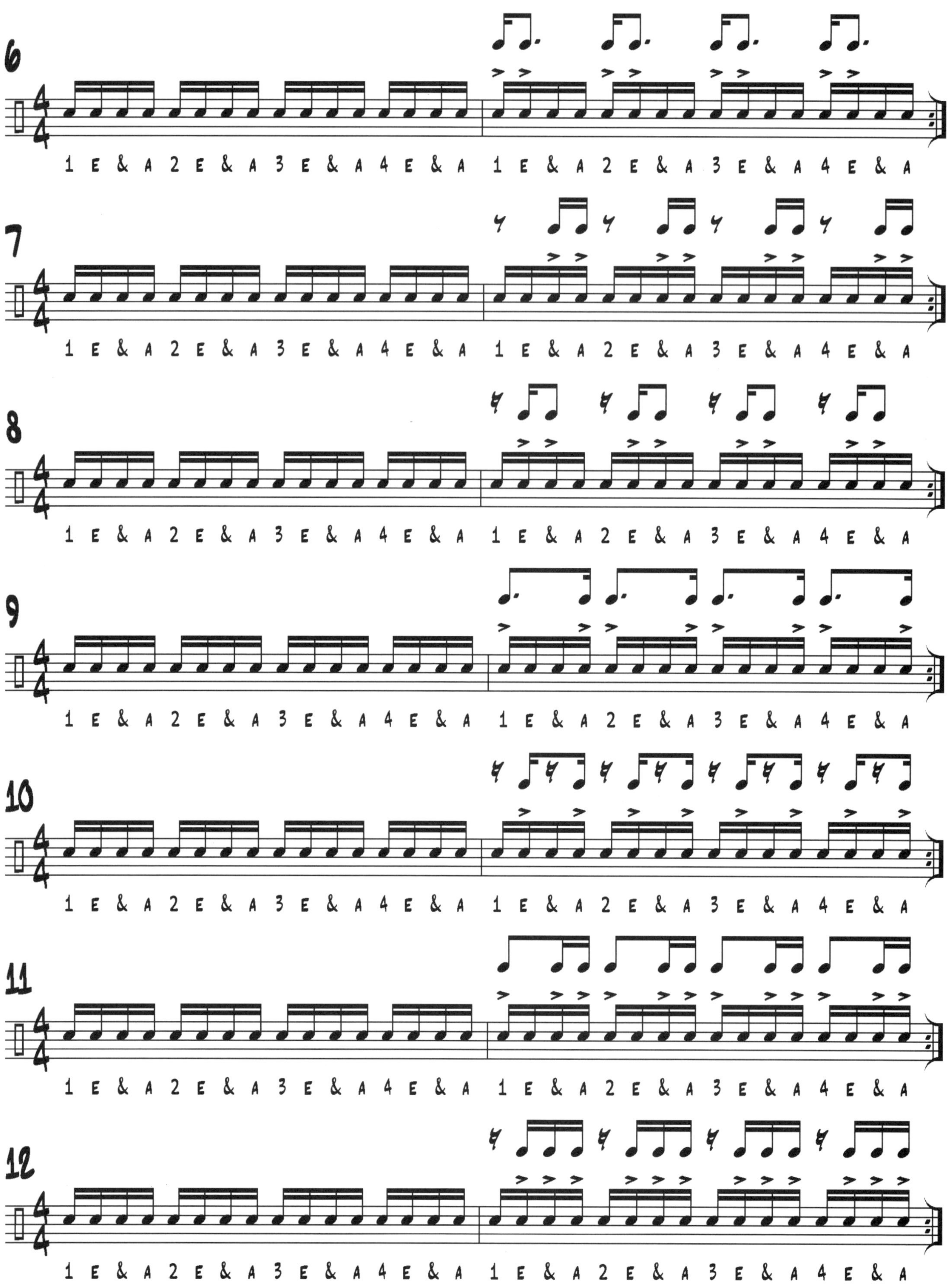

6
4/4
1 E & A 2 E & A 3 E & A 4 E & A   1 E & A 2 E & A 3 E & A 4 E & A
7
4/4
1 E & A 2 E & A 3 E & A 4 E & A   1 E & A 2 E & A 3 E & A 4 E & A
8
4/4
1 E & A 2 E & A 3 E & A 4 E & A   1 E & A 2 E & A 3 E & A 4 E & A
9
4/4
1 E & A 2 E & A 3 E & A 4 E & A   1 E & A 2 E & A 3 E & A 4 E & A
10
4/4
1 E & A 2 E & A 3 E & A 4 E & A   1 E & A 2 E & A 3 E & A 4 E & A
11
4/4
1 E & A 2 E & A 3 E & A 4 E & A   1 E & A 2 E & A 3 E & A 4 E & A
12
4/4
1 E & A 2 E & A 3 E & A 4 E & A   1 E & A 2 E & A 3 E & A 4 E & A

13
1 E & A 2 E & A 3 E & A 4 E & A 1 E & A 2 E & A 3 E & A 4 E & A
14
1 E & A 2 E & A 3 E & A 4 E & A 1 E & A 2 E & A 3 E & A 4 E & A
15
1 E & A 2 E & A 3 E & A 4 E & A 1 E & A 2 E & A 3 E & A 4 E & A

1c. Sixteenth-Note Element Combo Exercise

This exercise takes the accented Elements in ex. 1b and puts them together. Be sure to use your metronome and play this with accurate accents and non-accents, with a smooth flow.

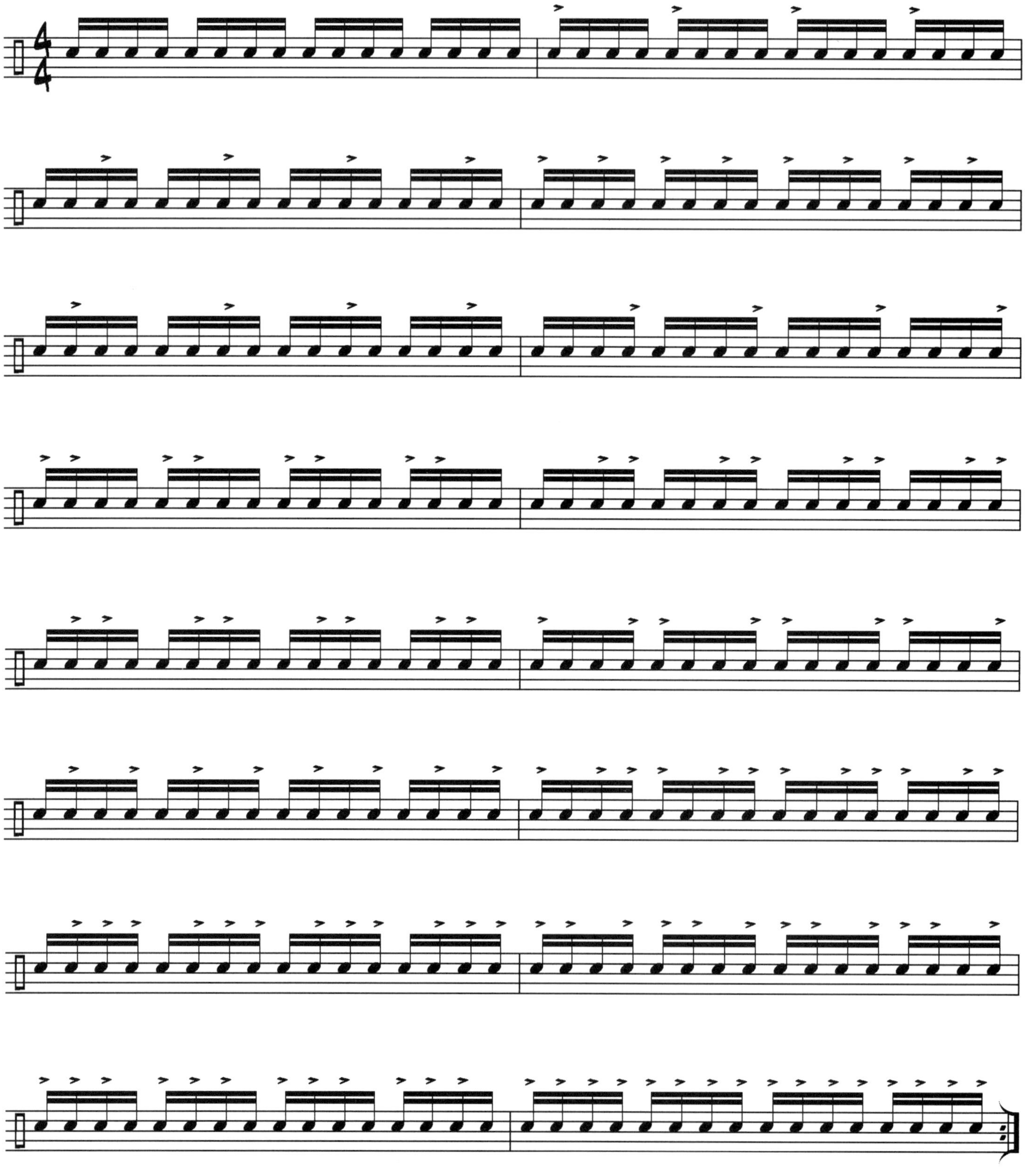

2a. Element Improvisation 1

The following exercise is an example of Elements improvised as accents in a sixteenth-note flow. I improvised these accents while thinking of various Elements and letting them come out naturally. Try to play this exercise with the unaccented notes as low strokes and the Elements (the accents) as full strokes. Make sure to keep a steady flow of low-stroke 16th-notes going.

When you are comfortable with this, improvise your own Elements as accents while playing sixteenths.

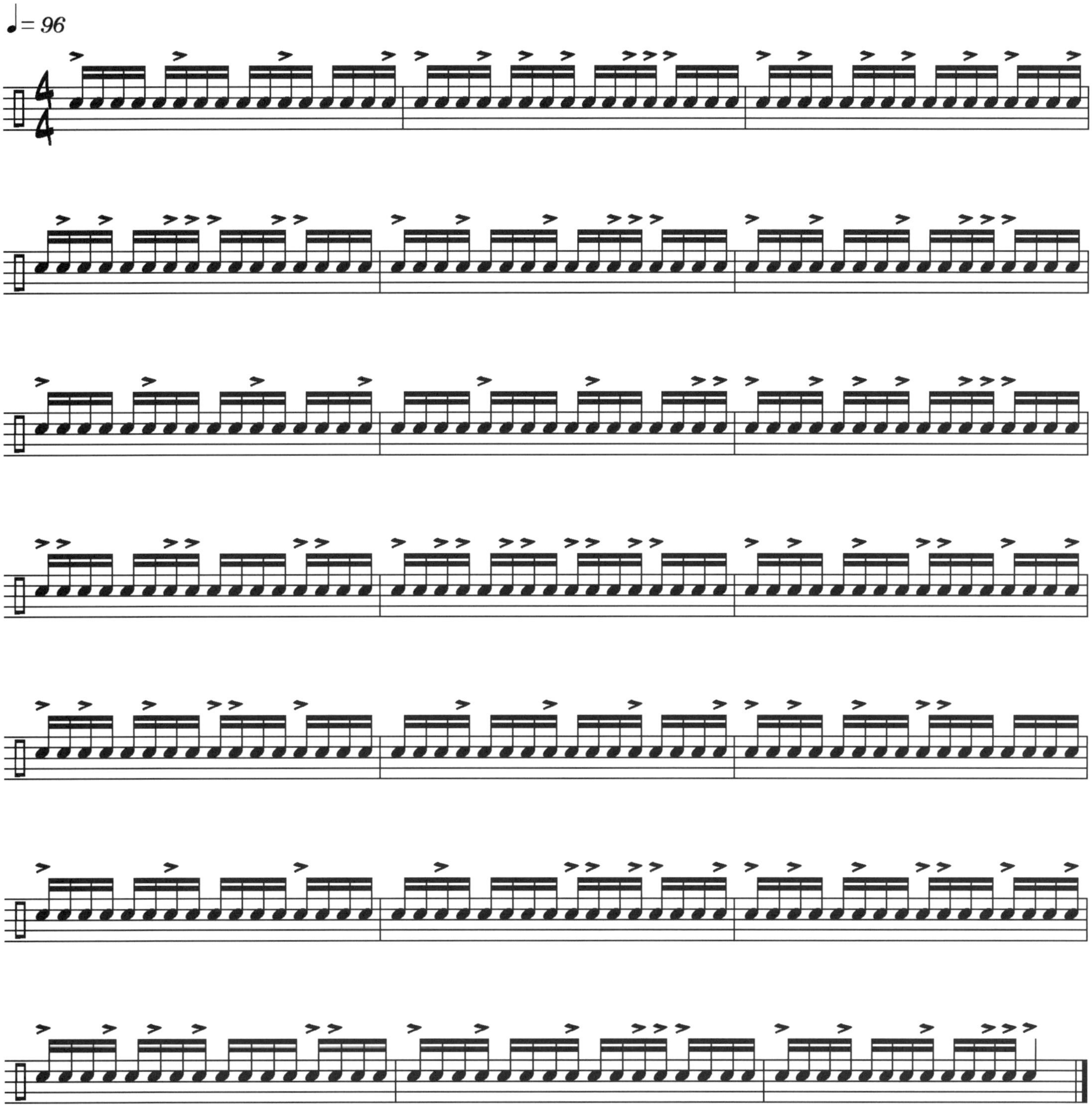

2b. Element Improvisation 2

Below is another example of accented Elements improvised over sixteenth-note low strokes, this time at a slightly faster tempo. Keep in mind that I improvised and recorded these ideas and then transcribed them, not the reverse. Your ultimate goal is to memorize the Elements and let them come out naturally in your playing in an improvisational way.

When you are comfortable with this, improvise your own Elements as accents while playing sixteenths.

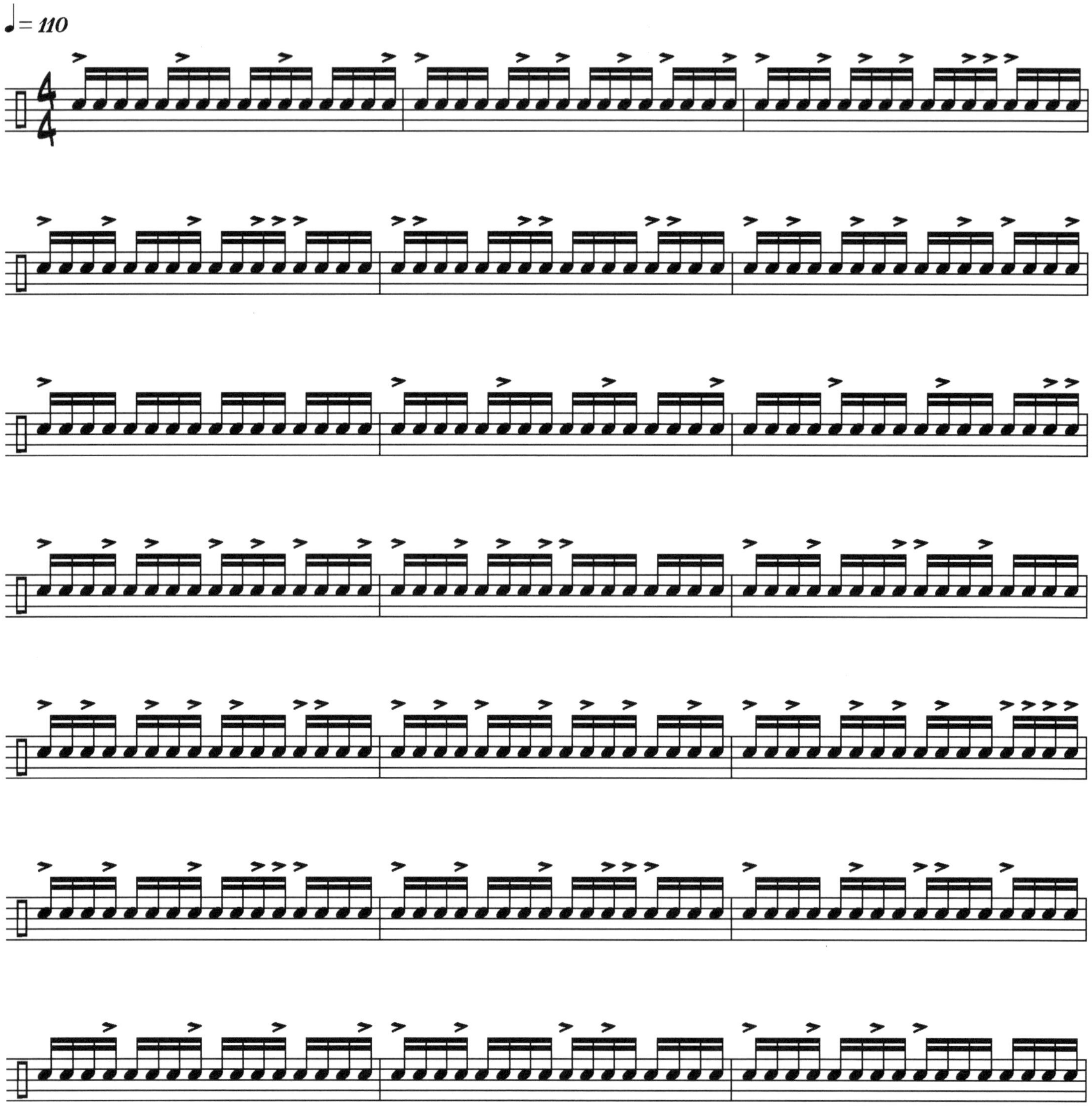

Dharma All-Stars at the Port Jeff Music Festival, Port Jefferson, NY
L to R: Bill Heller, Carl Fischer, Chieli Minucci, John Favicchia, Jack Knight, John Scarpulla

2c. Element Improvisation 3

Here is another example of accented Elements improvised over sixteenth-note low strokes, slightly faster than the previous two. These accented Element patterns can be played on pad, snare drum, or any surface of the drumset. Try playing the accents on a tom or cymbal and keeping the non-accents on the snare. This will prepare you for some of the material in the upcoming chapters.

When you are comfortable with this, improvise your own Elements as accents while playing sixteenths.

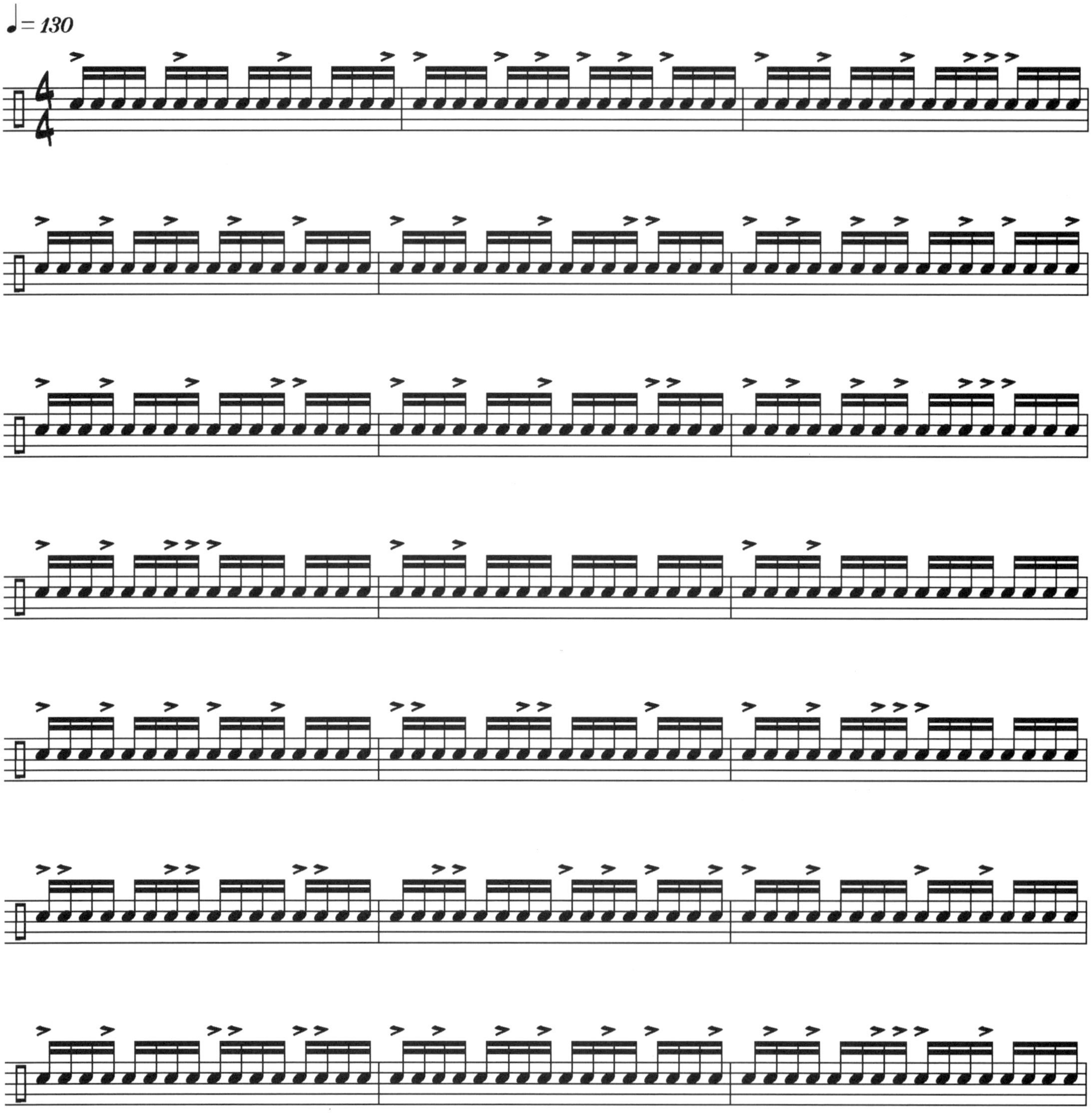

CD Track 6

2d. Element Improvisation 4

This exercise builds on the previous Element Improvisations by moving the accented Elements to various other surfaces on the drumset. By orchestrating the Elements in this way, you get your first glimpse of how understanding and applying Elements around the kit can make your playing much more interesting!

First, play this exercise as written, then improvise your own Elements and orchestrate them on your kit. To do this, you must improvise on two levels: 1) which Elements you are going to accent, and 2) on which part of the drumset you are going to play them. Try to play this exercise for as long as you can without stopping. If you stumble or break the flow, stop and start again from the beginning. Also keep in mind that this is a vocabulary builder. Some of these ideas are going to feel right and some will not. As you play, remember what feels and sounds right. Store these ideas away in your memory to be used again in the future. The ones that don't feel and sound good? Just forget them. Be open to experimenting and letting yourself just play without too much thought.

CD Track 7

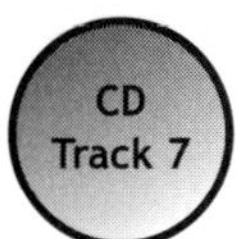

2e. Element Improvisation 5

This exercise is another example of combining the 16th-note Elements with improvised voicings around the kit.

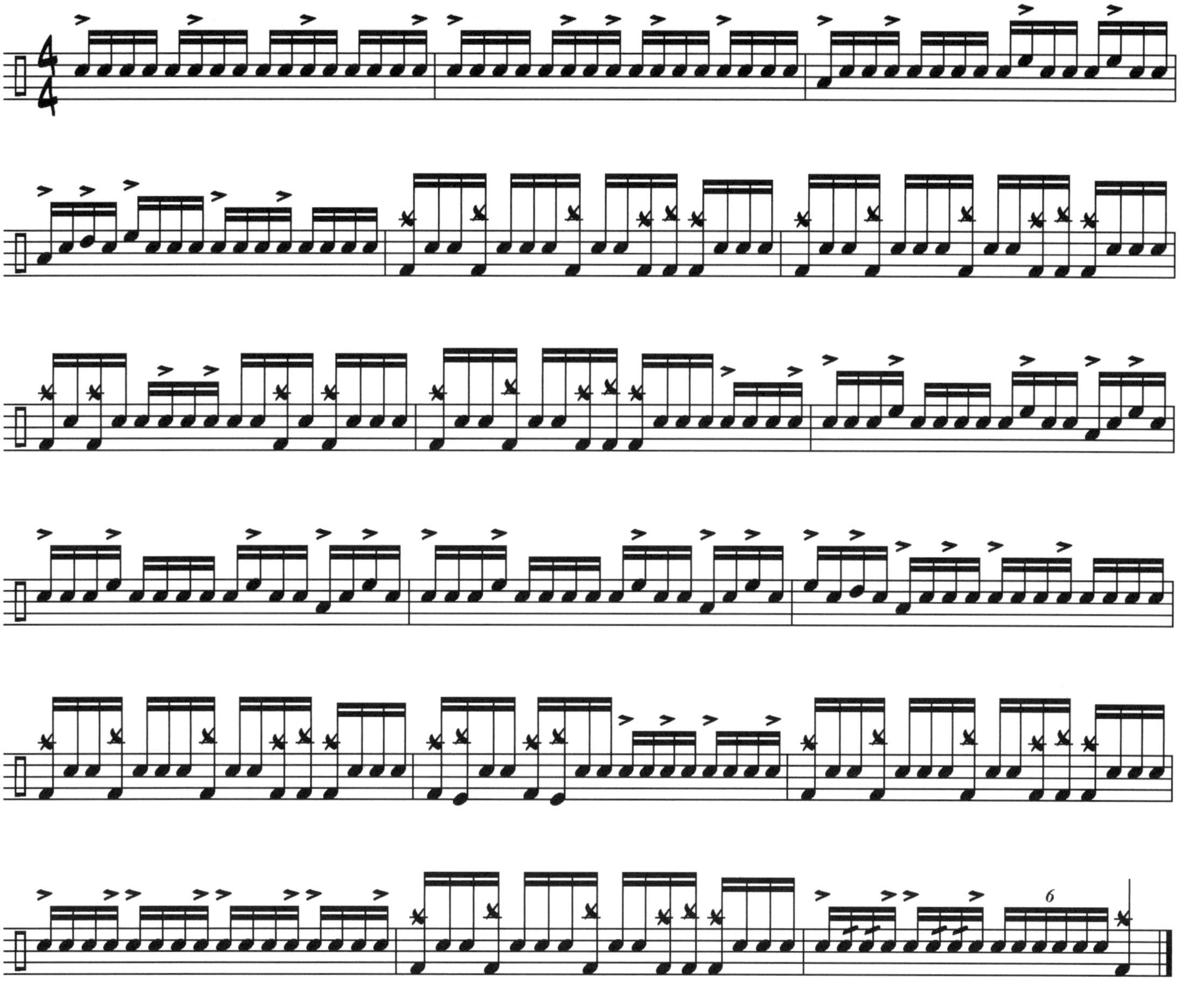

3. Accented Element Rolls: Intro

This section is similar to section 1, except that this time we will insert accented Elements into a flow of sixteenth-note open rolls. Play the roll as low strokes (2-3") and the accents as half strokes (6-9"). Be certain that when you accent the notes of the Element, that each accent is a *single* stroke, not a double! The ability to execute clean single-stroke accents while playing a roll in between is very important.

This exercise also helps in counting rolls. Now you can use rolls in your grooves and solos and not get lost!

As written: As played:

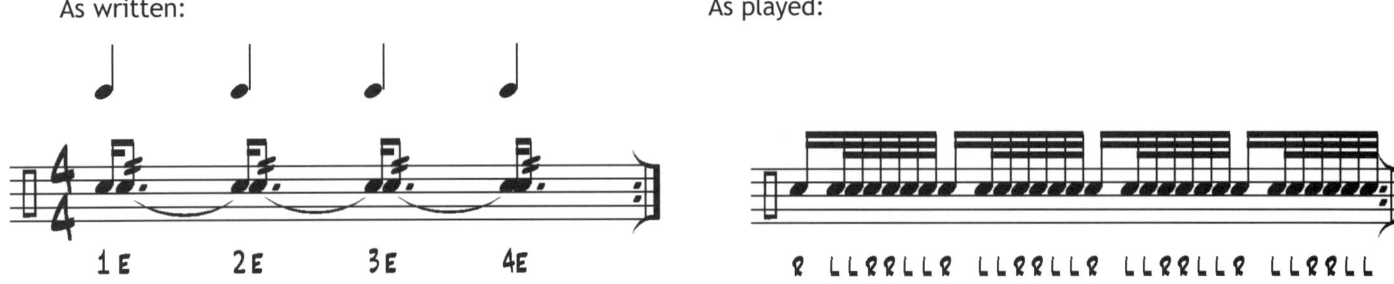

3a. Accented Element Rolls

CD Track 8

For this routine play an even 16th-note roll and accent each Element. Use a single sound surface and be sure to practice with a metronome to make sure your roll does not speed up or slow down.

7
1 & A 2 & A 3 & A 4 & A
8
1 E & A 2 E & A 3 E & A 4 E & A
9
1 E A 2 E A 3 E A 4 E A
10
1 E & A 2 E & A 3 E & A 4 E & A
11
1 E & A 2 E & A 3 E & A 4 E & A
12
1 E & A 2 E & A 3 E & A 4 E & A
13
1 E & A 2 E & A 3 E & A 4 E & A
14
1 E & A 2 E & A 3 E & A 4 E & A
15
1 E & A 2 E & A 3 E & A 4 E & A

CD Track 9

3b. 16th-Note Element Rolls Improvisation #1

The next step is to play a 16th-note open roll and then randomly insert Elements as single-stroke accents. First try playing my written example of this, and then improvise your own. Keep your ears open for melodies that the Elements make and let the melodies guide you as you improvise.

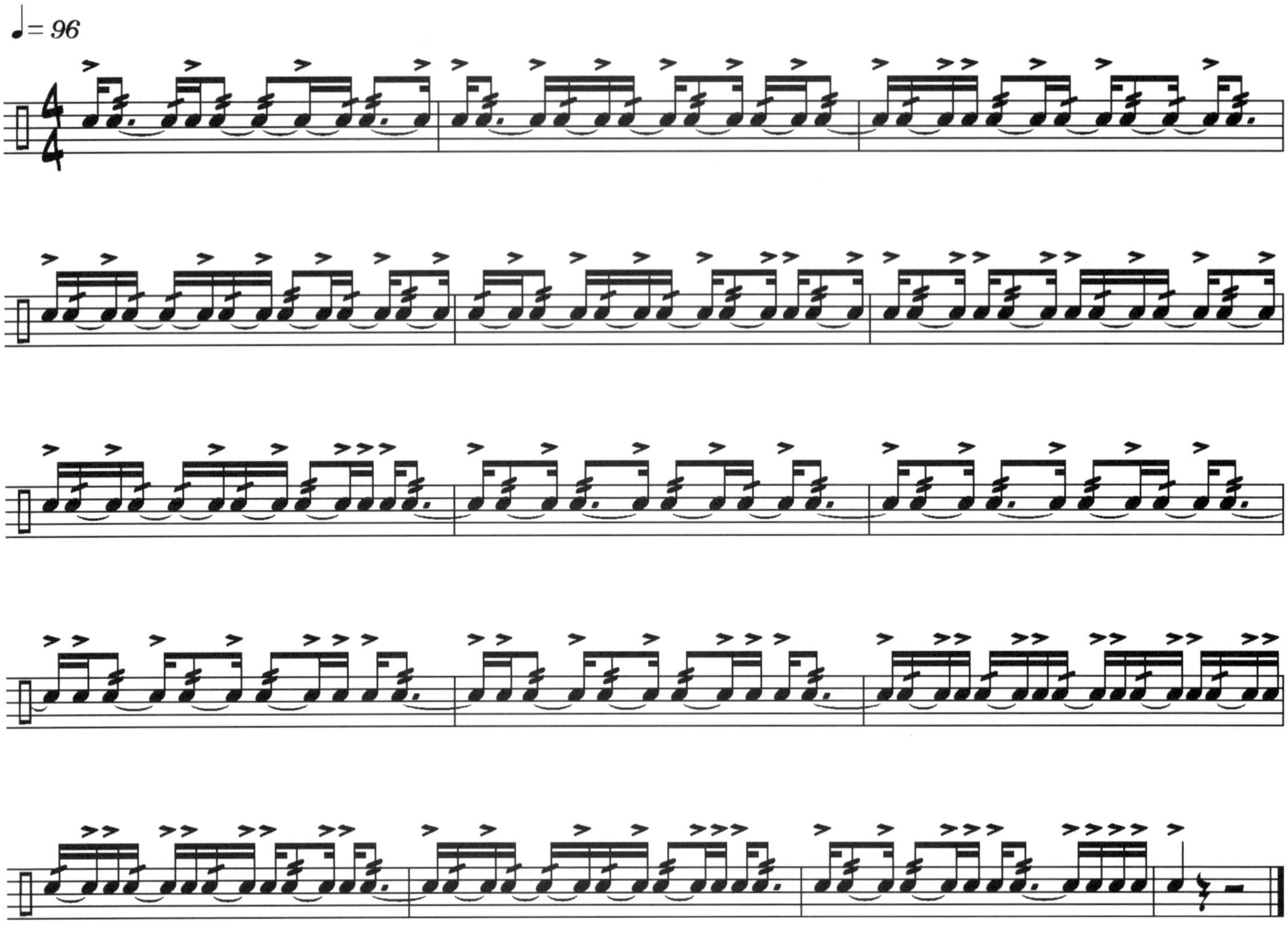

3c. 16th-Note Element Rolls Improvisation #2

3d. 16th-Note Element Rolls Improvisation #3

3e. Improvisation with Improvised Voicings

Now let's take our ability to play 16th-note open rolls with improvised Elements and apply it to the drumset. In the improvised example below, I orchestrated Elements all over the kit and kept the roll flow going on my snare drum.

First, play this exercise as written; then improvise your own Elements and orchestrate them on your kit. To do this, you must improvise on two levels: 1) which Elements you are going to accent, and 2) on which part of the drumset you are going to play them. Try to play this exercise for as long as you can without stopping. If you stumble or break the flow, stop and start again from the beginning. Also keep in mind that this is a vocabulary builder. Some of these ideas are going to feel right and some will not. As you play, remember what feels and sounds right. Store these ideas away in your memory to be used again in the future. The ones that don't feel and sound good? Just forget them. Be open to experimenting and letting yourself just play without too much thought.

4. 16th-Note Element Application: Three Bars of Time and a One-Bar Fill

In this routine you will play three bars of any 8th-note or 16th-note-based groove, followed by a one-bar fill. For the fill, think of an Element and orchestrate it on the kit. Your job is to voice the Element in the most musical way possible. Try to think of as many Elements as possible, and use them as the basis for your fill. Use a metronome so that your fills don't speed up or slow down.

After you play though the entire exercise many times, the next step is to combine Elements when you fill. If you can make one Element in a fill sound good, then once you start to mix and match all the Elements you will be on your way to making your vocabulary larger and larger.

The next two pages contain of all the Element variations to practice.

For example, using the following Element as a fill:

You might orchestrate it in the following ways:

4a. One-Bar Fills Using 16th-Note Elements

1 PLAY TIME

1 E & A 2 E & A 3 E & A 4 E & A

2 PLAY TIME

1 E & A 2 E & A 3 E & A 4 E & A

3 PLAY TIME

1 E & A 2 E & A 3 E & A 4 E & A

4 PLAY TIME

1 E & A 2 E & A 3 E & A 4 E & A

5 PLAY TIME

1 E & A 2 E & A 3 E & A 4 E & A

6 PLAY TIME

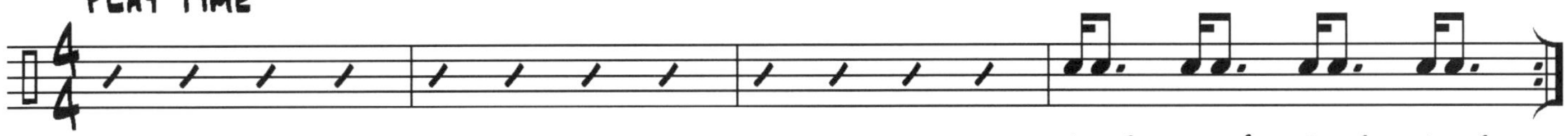

1 E & A 2 E & A 3 E & A 4 E & A

7 PLAY TIME

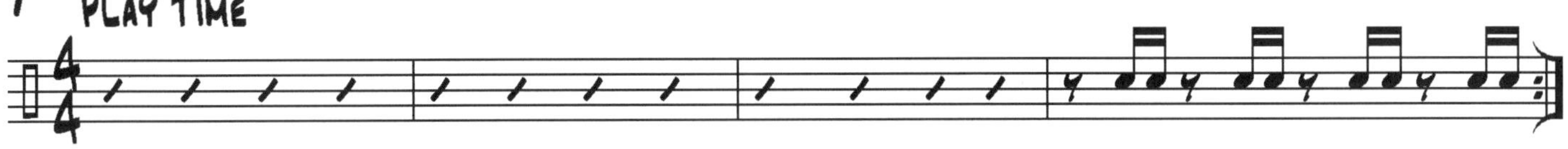

1 E & A 2 E & A 3 E & A 4 E & A

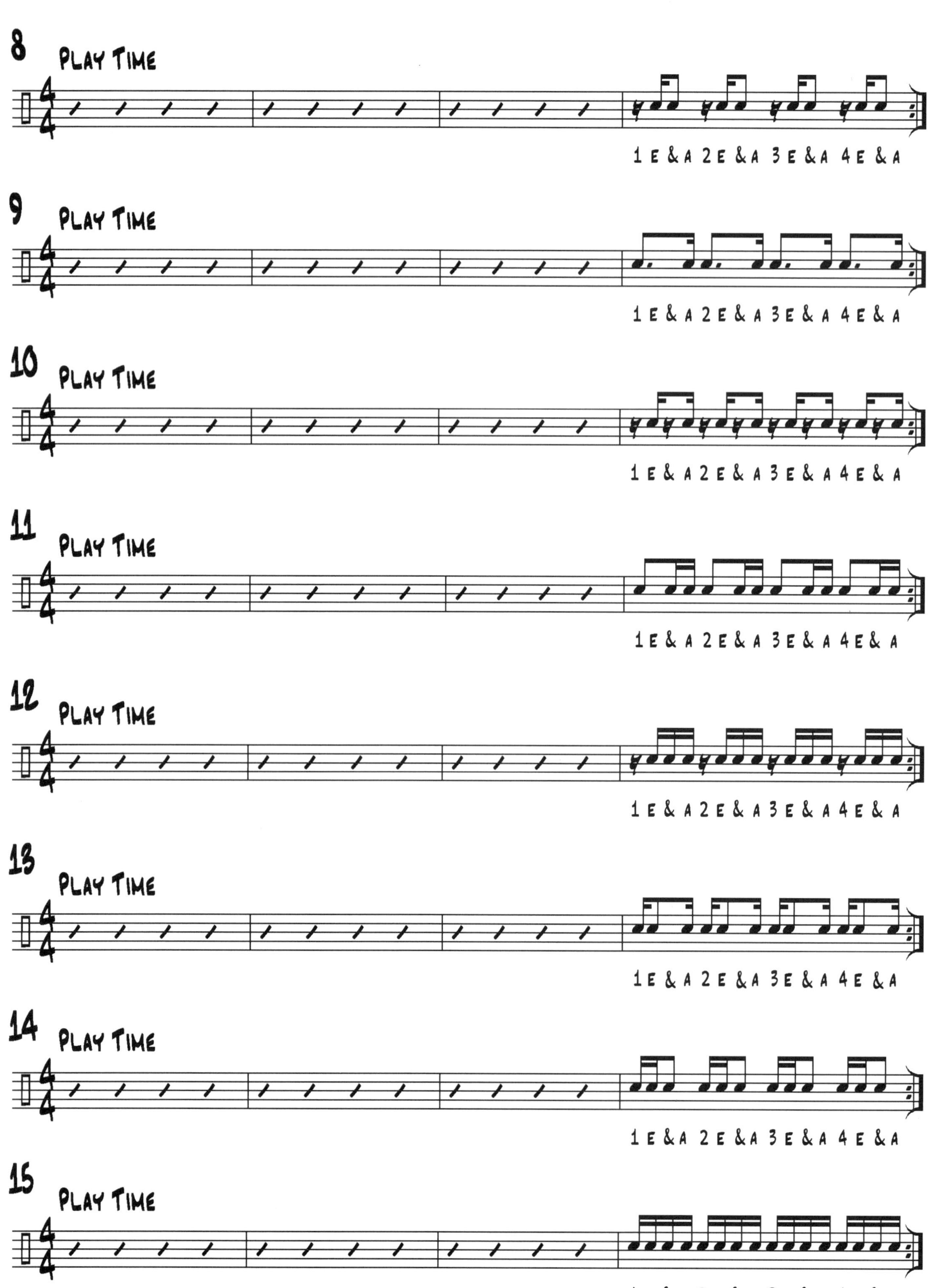
8 PLAY TIME
1 E & A 2 E & A 3 E & A 4 E & A
9 PLAY TIME
1 E & A 2 E & A 3 E & A 4 E & A
10 PLAY TIME
1 E & A 2 E & A 3 E & A 4 E & A
11 PLAY TIME
1 E & A 2 E & A 3 E & A 4 E & A
12 PLAY TIME
1 E & A 2 E & A 3 E & A 4 E & A
13 PLAY TIME
1 E & A 2 E & A 3 E & A 4 E & A
14 PLAY TIME
1 E & A 2 E & A 3 E & A 4 E & A
15 PLAY TIME
1 E & A 2 E & A 3 E & A 4 E & A

5. Additional Applications

Random Voicing Exercise 1

Now that you have practiced the Elements with the previously outlined routines, you should spend some time improvising with the Elements.

Take each Element one at a time and voice it around the kit for as long as you can without stopping or repeating yourself. The goal is to be able to play the Element for up to five minutes and keep it musical and interesting. At first you might find yourself falling back on the same ideas over and over again. Push yourself to continue practicing until you can improvise with each Element more freely, without repeating the same orchestrations. Once you can play each Element in this way, your vocabulary will be elevated to the next level.

Random Voicing Exercise 2

Count 16th notes out loud and play any Element at random on any voice. This will help to develop your inner clock as well as further your ability to improvise orchestrations and placement of the Elements.

John with the Dharma All-Stars at the IMAC Theater,
Huntington, NY, 2006

CD Track 16 96 bpm

CD Track 17 130 bpm

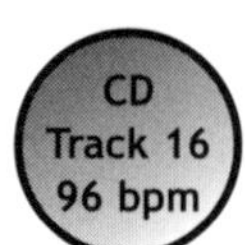

6a. Ensemble Playing 1:

16th-Note Element Ensemble Hits on Beat 1

In addition to expanding your vocabulary on the drumset, understanding the Elements will also help you to execute rhythms played within the musical ensemble. All ensemble figures encountered on charts can be broken down into the Elements you have already learned.

Ensemble hits were very popular with Big Bands and Latin bands but in more recent times have become part of all musical styles. This section presents ensemble figure exercises for you to practice. This first set of exercises presents all the Elements one at a time, occuring on beat 1 of the bar. The next set moves all the Elements back to beat 2, then beat 3, and beat 4. When you have mastered these exercises, you will easily be able to catch any one-beat 16th-note-based ensemble hit in any position in the bar.

Each track has two bars of time up front. You will then play one bar of time with a fill leading into an ensemble figure in the second bar. Try playing the hits with two basic interpretations. First, play them wih "long" sounds (i.e., a cymbal crash), and then with "short" sounds (i.e., a snare accent or other staccato sound).

1 Repeat 4x (2 Bars Click up Front)

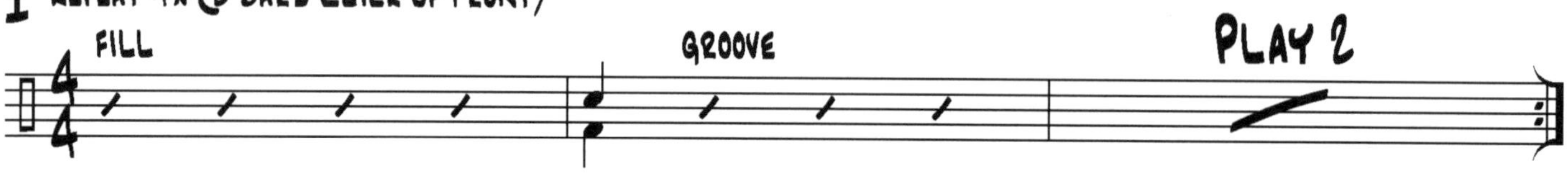

2 Repeat 4x

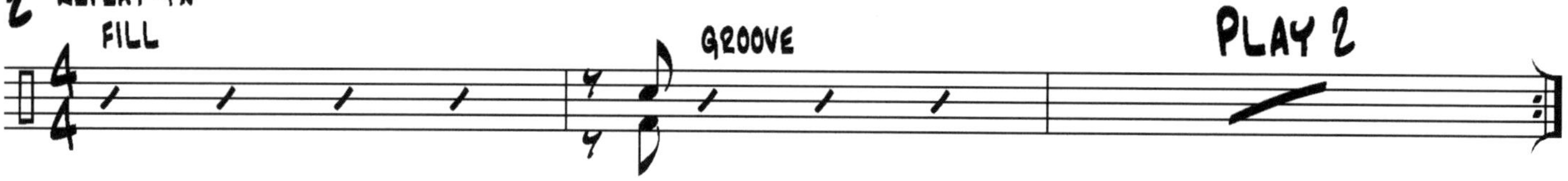

3 Repeat 4x

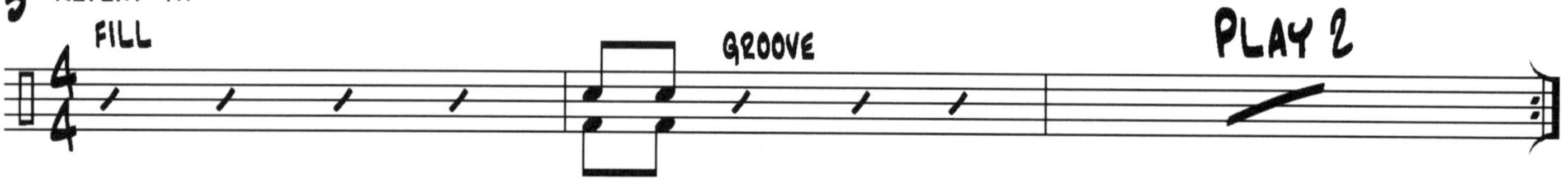

4 Repeat 4x

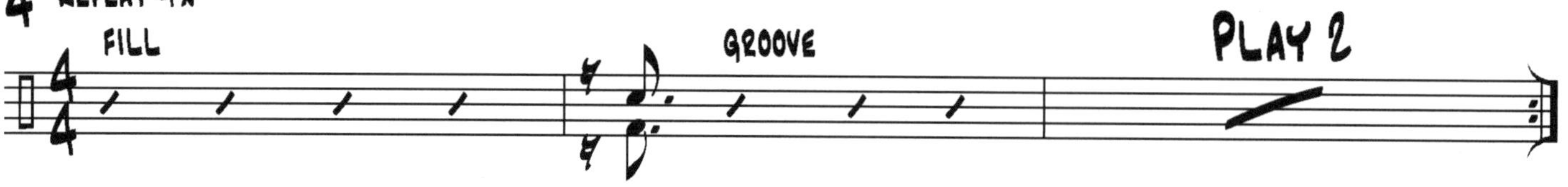

5 Repeat 4x

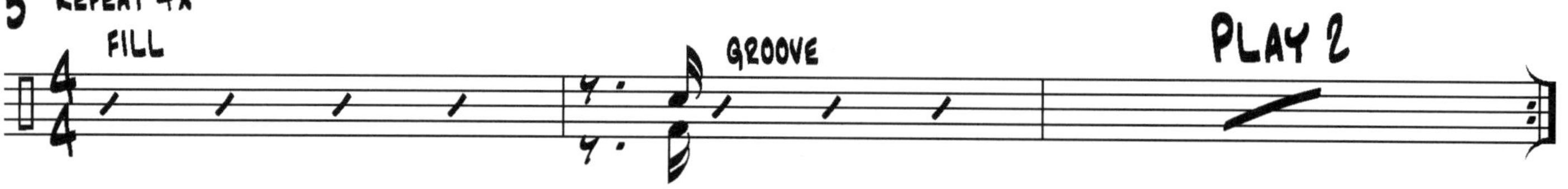

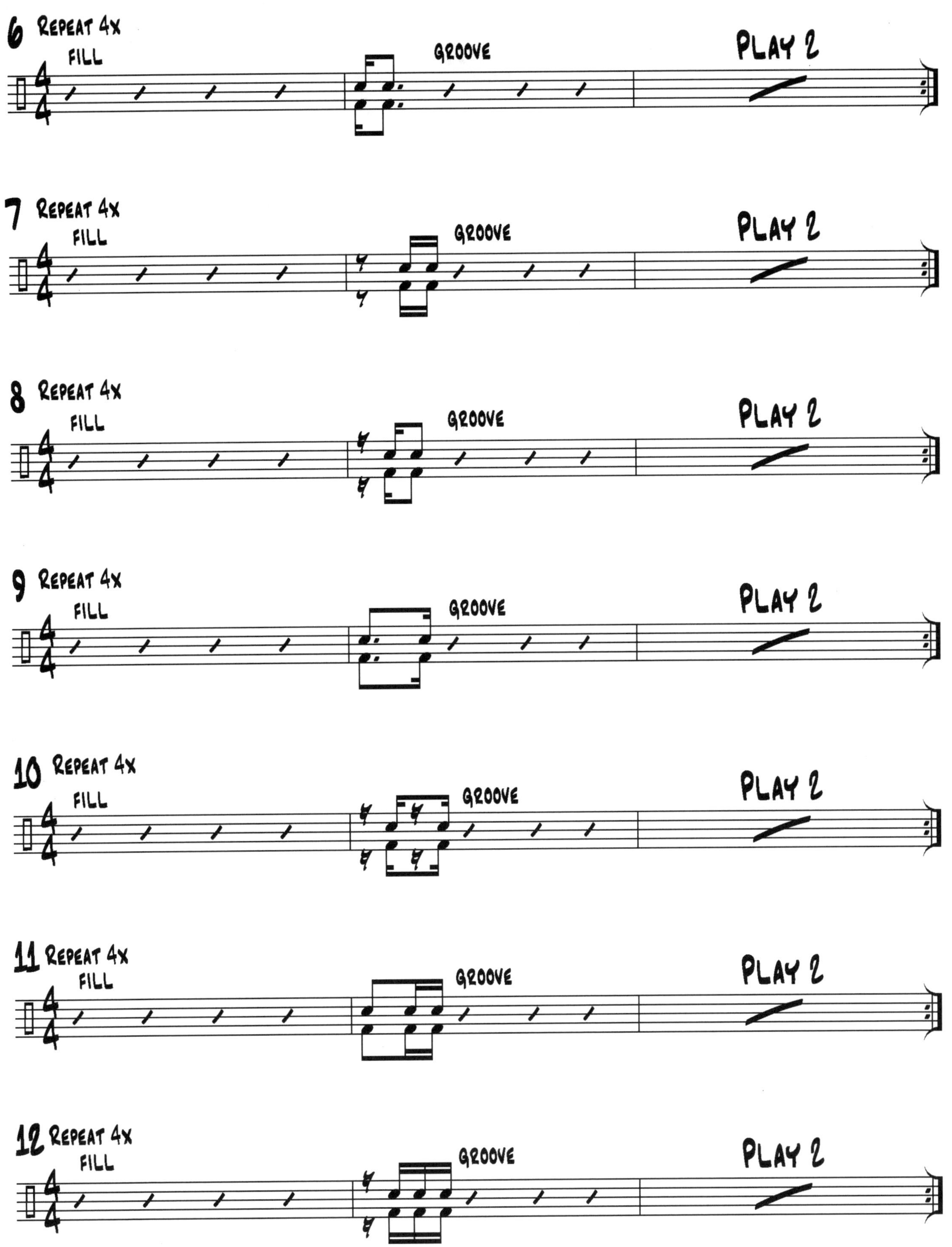
6 REPEAT 4x
FILL
GROOVE
PLAY 2

7 REPEAT 4x
FILL
GROOVE
PLAY 2

8 REPEAT 4x
FILL
GROOVE
PLAY 2

9 REPEAT 4x
FILL
GROOVE
PLAY 2

10 REPEAT 4x
FILL
GROOVE
PLAY 2

11 REPEAT 4x
FILL
GROOVE
PLAY 2

12 REPEAT 4x
FILL
GROOVE
PLAY 2

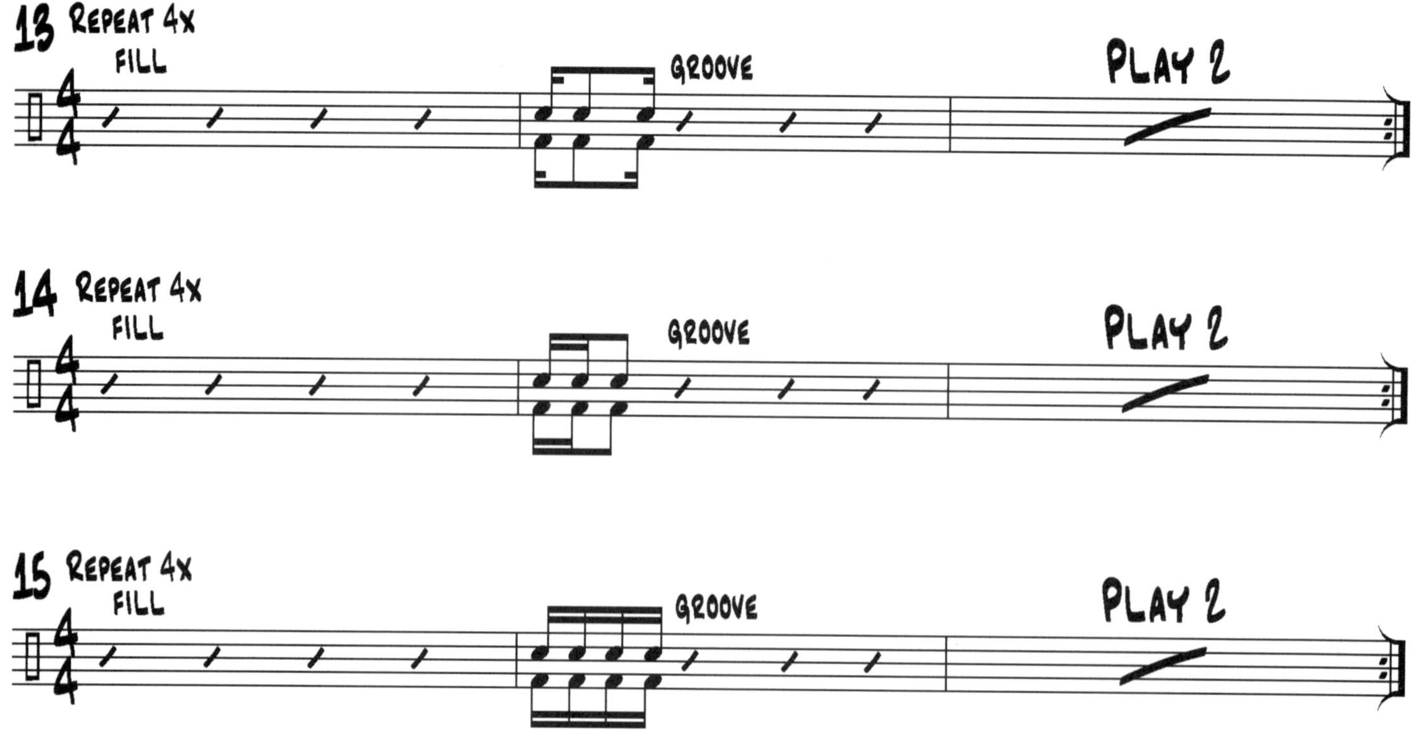

Jim Chapin and John Favicchia

CD Track 18 96 bpm

CD Track 19 130 bpm

6b. Ensemble Playing 1:

16th-Note Element Ensemble Hits on Beat 2

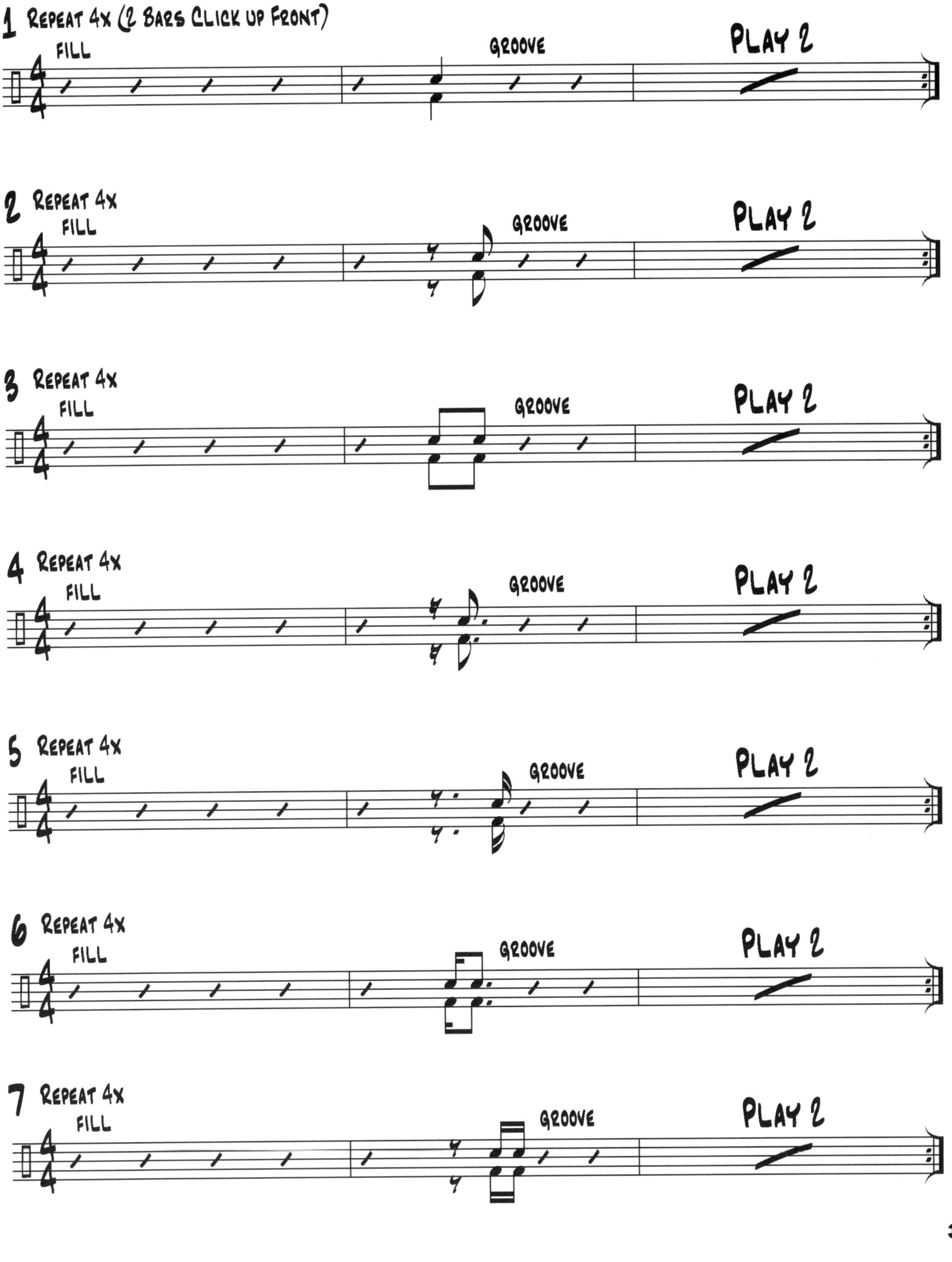

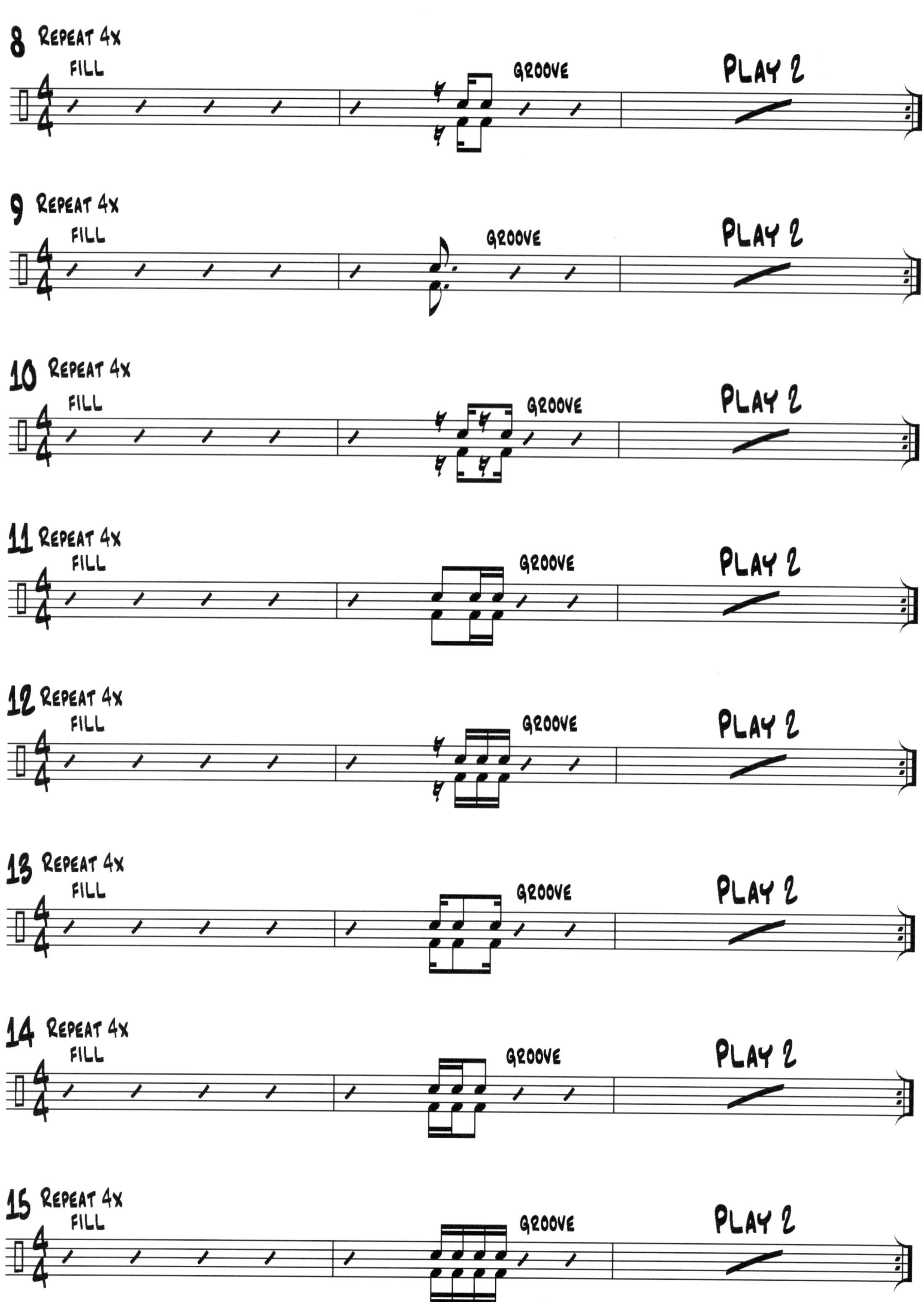

8 REPEAT 4x
FILL
GROOVE
PLAY 2

9 REPEAT 4x
FILL
GROOVE
PLAY 2

10 REPEAT 4x
FILL
GROOVE
PLAY 2

11 REPEAT 4x
FILL
GROOVE
PLAY 2

12 REPEAT 4x
FILL
GROOVE
PLAY 2

13 REPEAT 4x
FILL
GROOVE
PLAY 2

14 REPEAT 4x
FILL
GROOVE
PLAY 2

15 REPEAT 4x
FILL
GROOVE
PLAY 2

CD
Track 20
96 bpm

CD
Track 21
130 bpm

6c. Ensemble Playing 1:

16th-Note Element Ensemble Hits on Beat 3

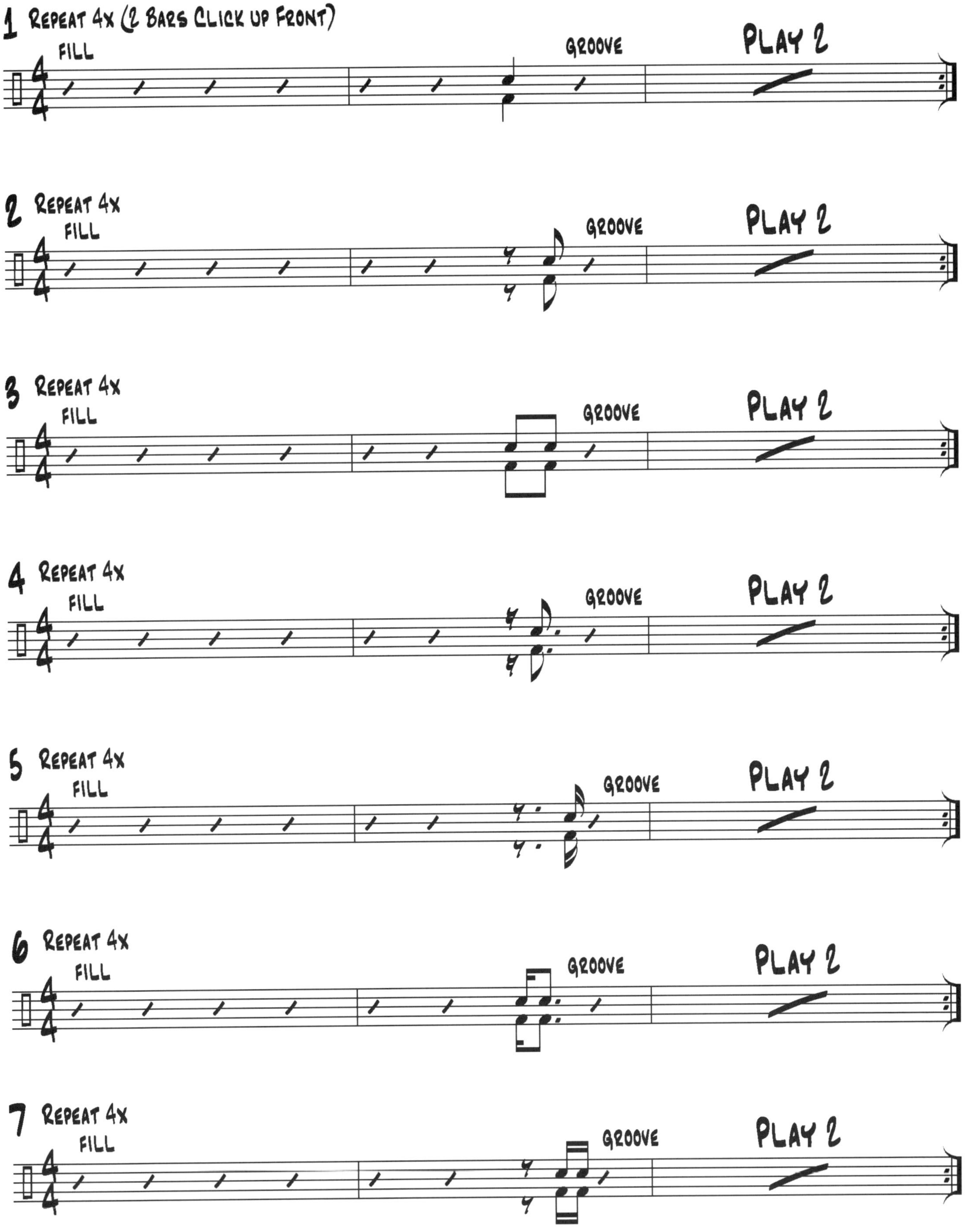

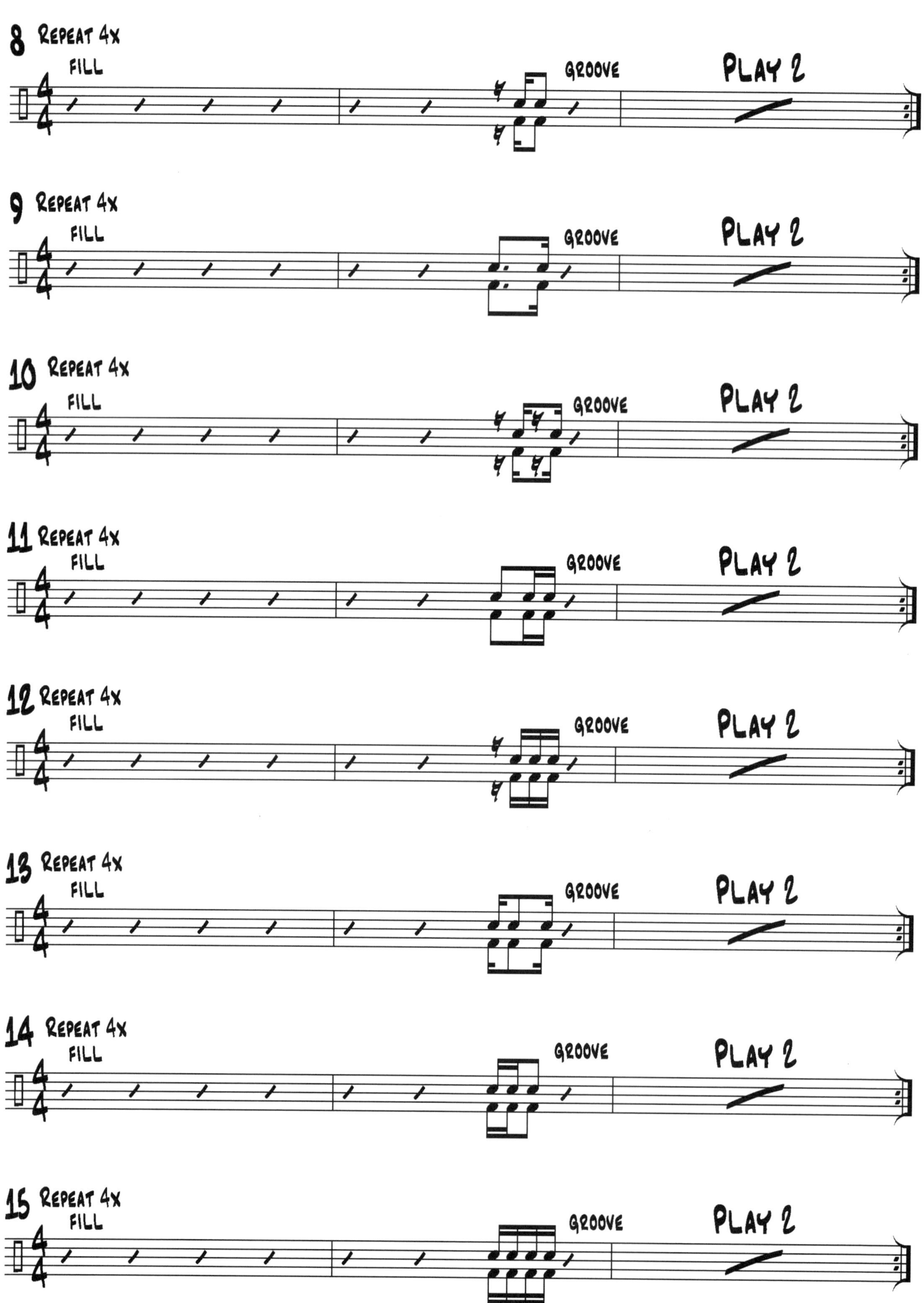
8 REPEAT 4x
FILL
GROOVE
PLAY 2
9 REPEAT 4x
FILL
GROOVE
PLAY 2
10 REPEAT 4x
FILL
GROOVE
PLAY 2
11 REPEAT 4x
FILL
GROOVE
PLAY 2
12 REPEAT 4x
FILL
GROOVE
PLAY 2
13 REPEAT 4x
FILL
GROOVE
PLAY 2
14 REPEAT 4x
FILL
GROOVE
PLAY 2
15 REPEAT 4x
FILL
GROOVE
PLAY 2

CD Track 22 96 bpm

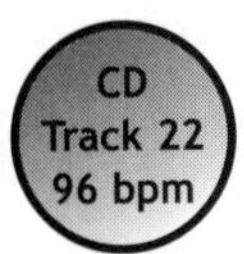

CD Track 23 130 bpm

6d. Ensemble Playing 1:

16th-Note Element Ensemble Hits on Beat 4

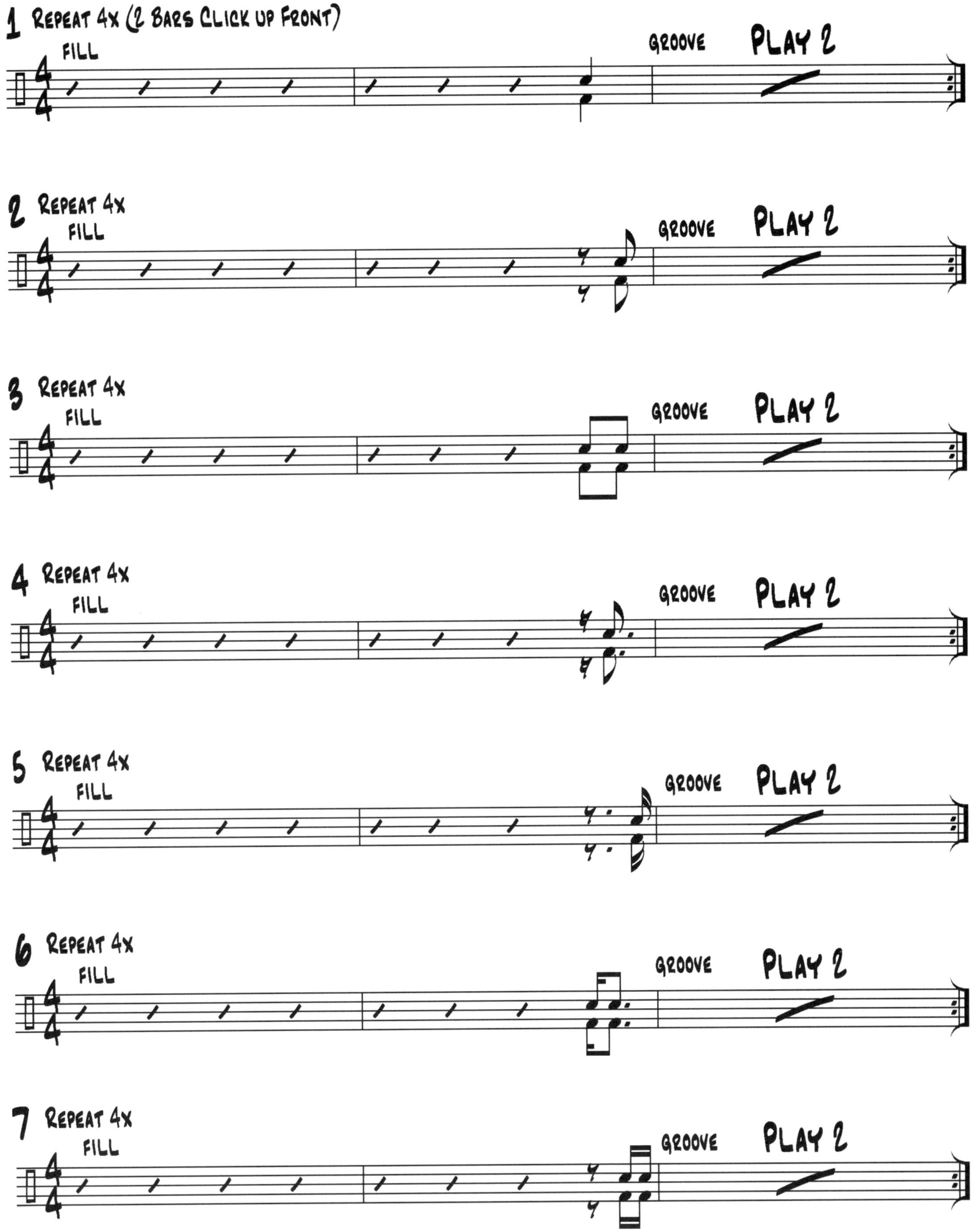
1 REPEAT 4X (2 BARS CLICK UP FRONT)
FILL
GROOVE
PLAY 2
2 REPEAT 4X
FILL
GROOVE
PLAY 2
3 REPEAT 4X
FILL
GROOVE
PLAY 2
4 REPEAT 4X
FILL
GROOVE
PLAY 2
5 REPEAT 4X
FILL
GROOVE
PLAY 2
6 REPEAT 4X
FILL
GROOVE
PLAY 2
7 REPEAT 4X
FILL
GROOVE
PLAY 2

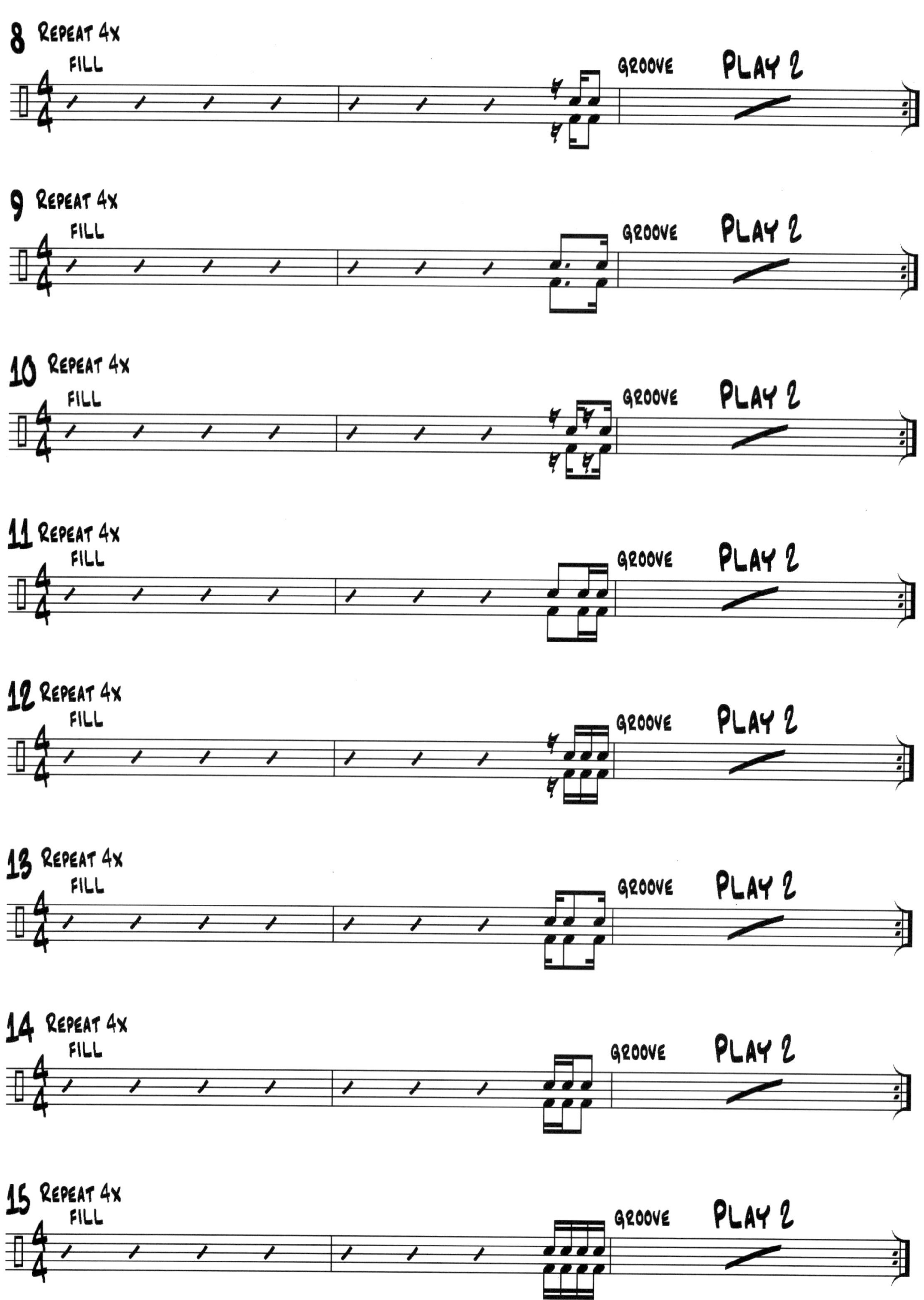

8 REPEAT 4x
FILL
GROOVE
PLAY 2

9 REPEAT 4x
FILL
GROOVE
PLAY 2

10 REPEAT 4x
FILL
GROOVE
PLAY 2

11 REPEAT 4x
FILL
GROOVE
PLAY 2

12 REPEAT 4x
FILL
GROOVE
PLAY 2

13 REPEAT 4x
FILL
GROOVE
PLAY 2

14 REPEAT 4x
FILL
GROOVE
PLAY 2

15 REPEAT 4x
FILL
GROOVE
PLAY 2

CD Track 16 96 bpm

CD Track 17 130 bpm

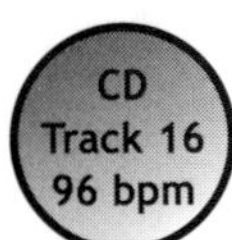

7a. Ensemble Playing 2:

16th-Note Element Ensemble Hits on Beat 1

Now that we have practiced catching the Elements as ensemble figures in the phrase, the next step is to practice soloing around the hits. The Elements in this example are the ensemble hits, and you will be soloing around them in a four-bar phrase. Each track on the CD has two bars of click up front, followed by a four-bar phrase containing an ensemble figure in the second bar. Use these tracks to practice catching the ensemble hits and/or soloing around them. This will ensure that your four-bar phrasing is accurate. Use the accented and roll Elements to give you ideas of solo figures to play around the hits.

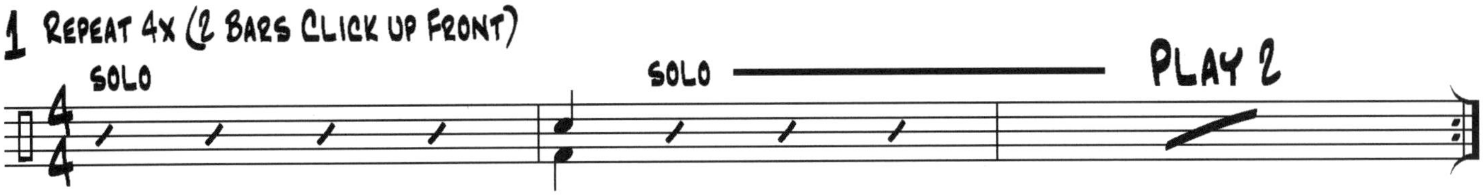

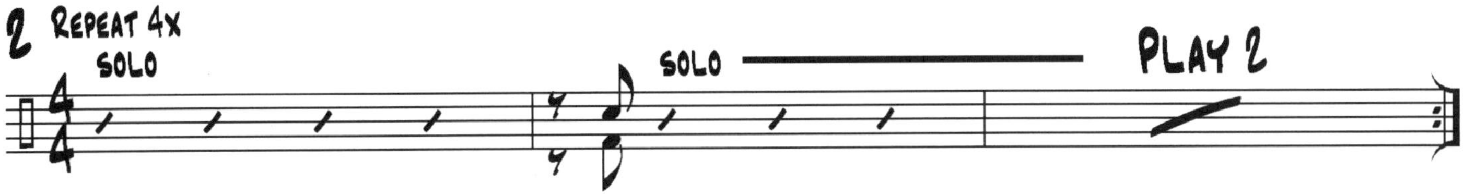

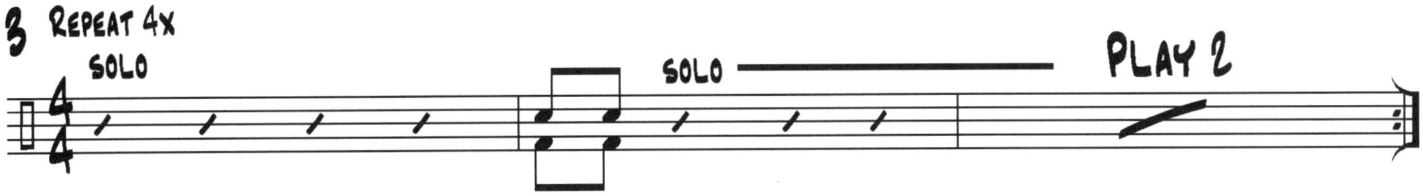

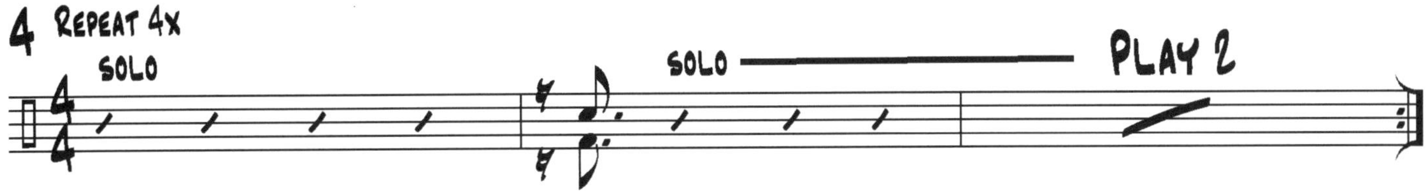

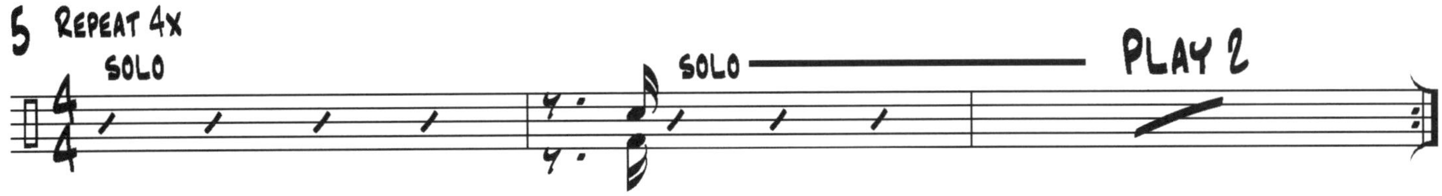

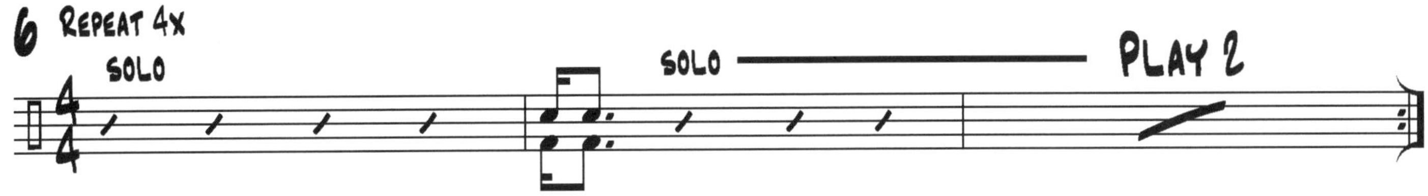

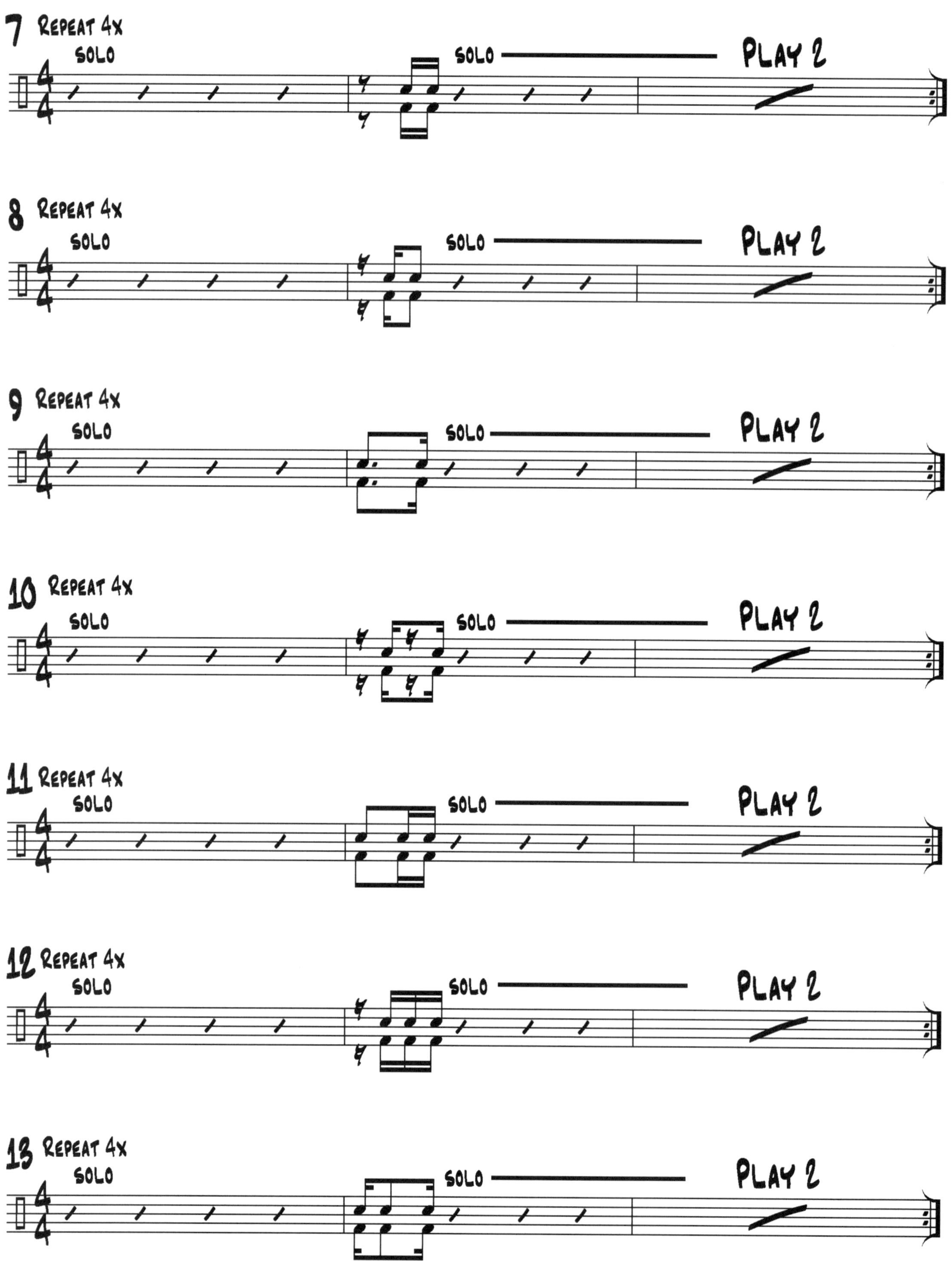
7 Repeat 4x
SOLO
SOLO
PLAY 2
8 Repeat 4x
SOLO
SOLO
PLAY 2
9 Repeat 4x
SOLO
SOLO
PLAY 2
10 Repeat 4x
SOLO
SOLO
PLAY 2
11 Repeat 4x
SOLO
SOLO
PLAY 2
12 Repeat 4x
SOLO
SOLO
PLAY 2
13 Repeat 4x
SOLO
SOLO
PLAY 2

14 REPEAT 4X
SOLO
SOLO
PLAY 2
4/4
15 REPEAT 4X
SOLO
SOLO
PLAY 2
4/4

7b. Ensemble Playing 2:

16th-Note Element Ensemble Hits on Beat 2

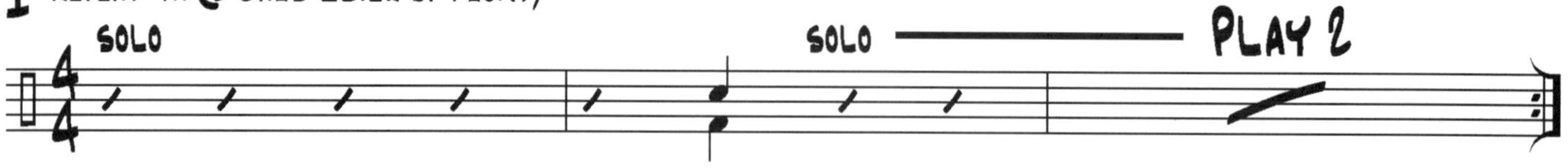

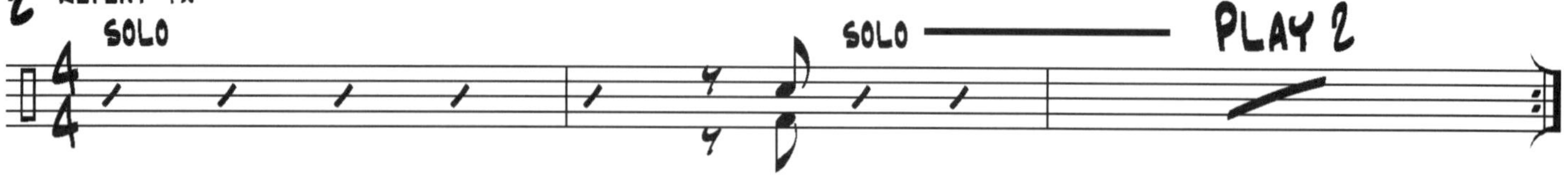

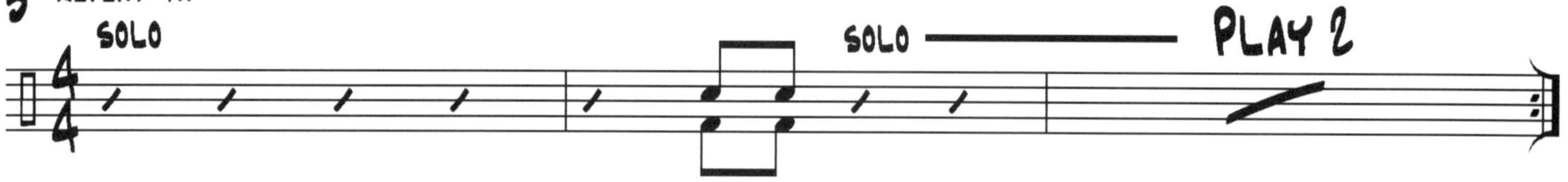

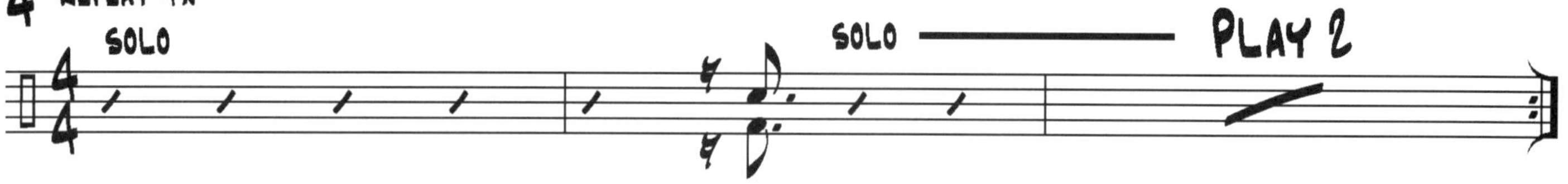

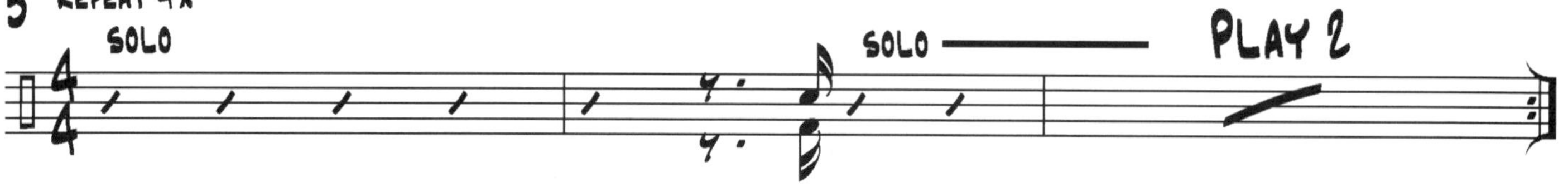

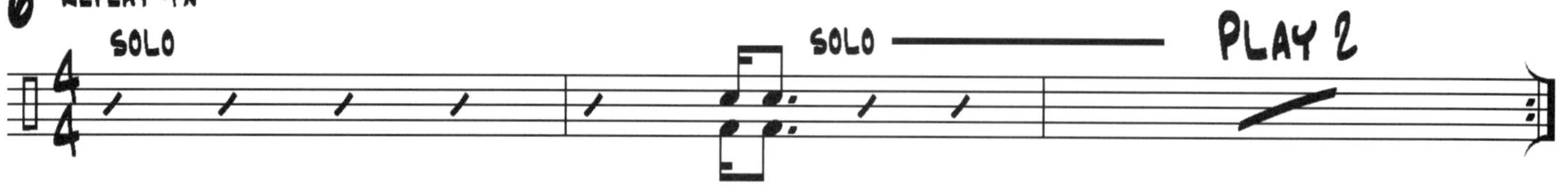

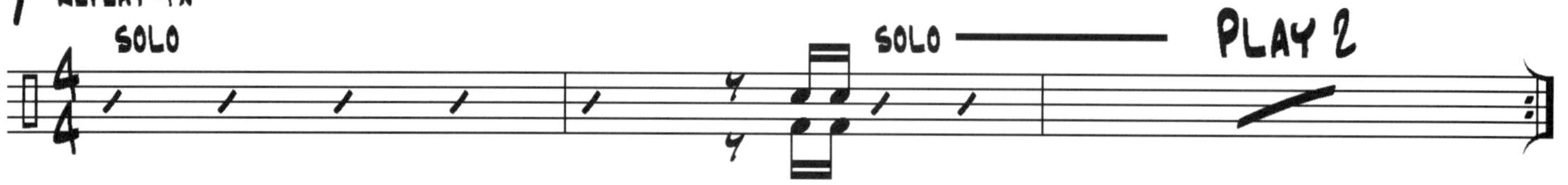

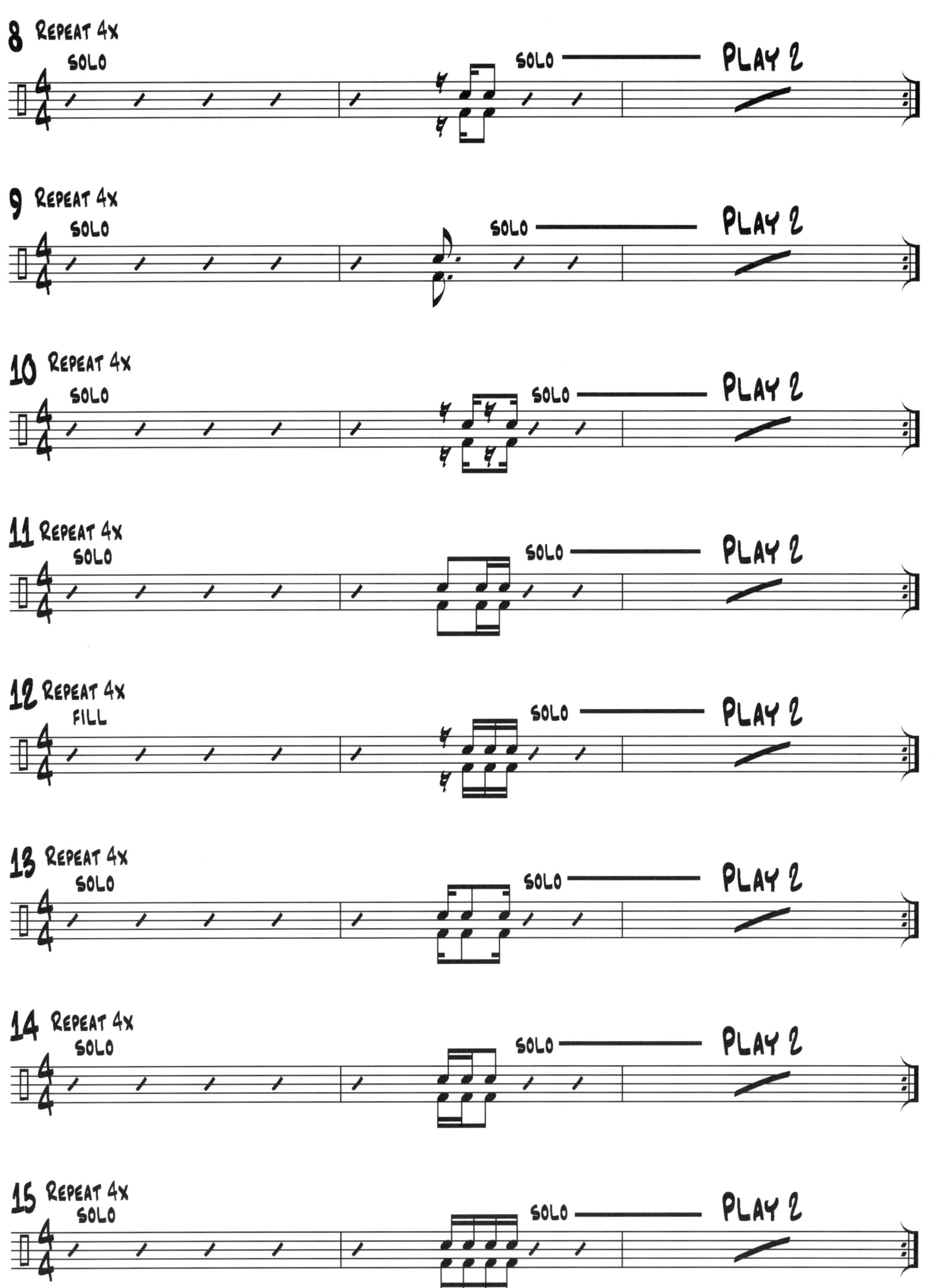
8 REPEAT 4x
SOLO
SOLO
PLAY 2

9 REPEAT 4x
SOLO
SOLO
PLAY 2

10 REPEAT 4x
SOLO
SOLO
PLAY 2

11 REPEAT 4x
SOLO
SOLO
PLAY 2

12 REPEAT 4x
FILL
SOLO
PLAY 2

13 REPEAT 4x
SOLO
SOLO
PLAY 2

14 REPEAT 4x
SOLO
SOLO
PLAY 2

15 REPEAT 4x
SOLO
SOLO
PLAY 2

CD Track 20 96 bpm

CD Track 21 130 bpm

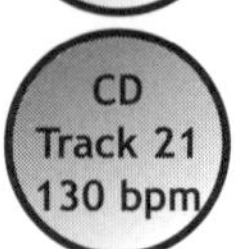

7c. Ensemble Playing 2:

16th-Note Element Ensemble Hits on Beat 3

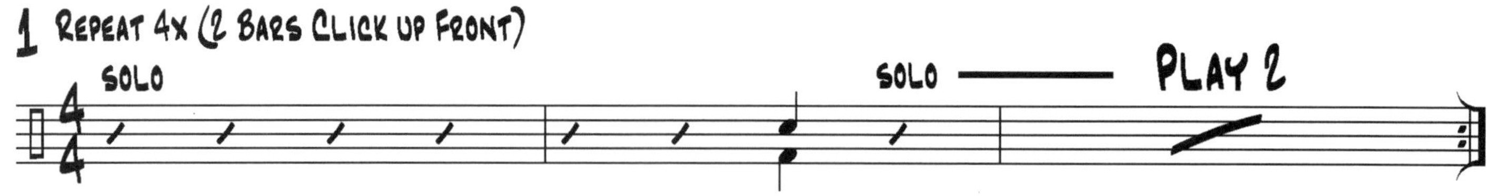
1 Repeat 4x (2 Bars Click up Front)
SOLO
SOLO
Play 2

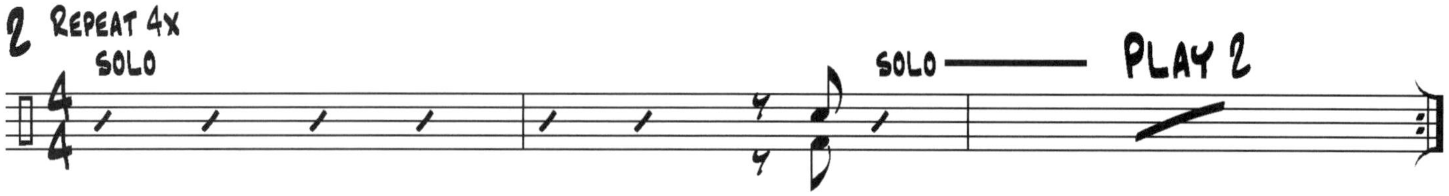
2 Repeat 4x
SOLO
SOLO
Play 2

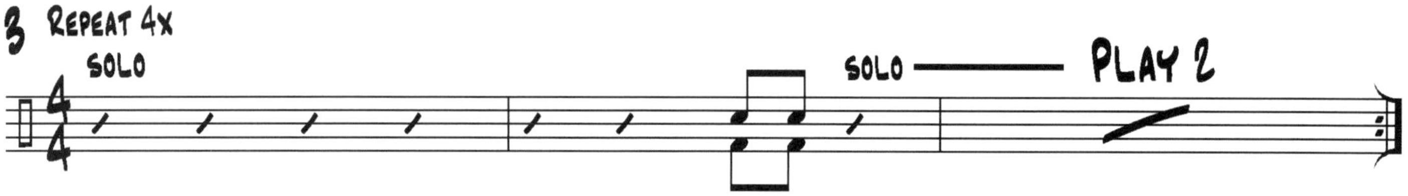
3 Repeat 4x
SOLO
SOLO
Play 2

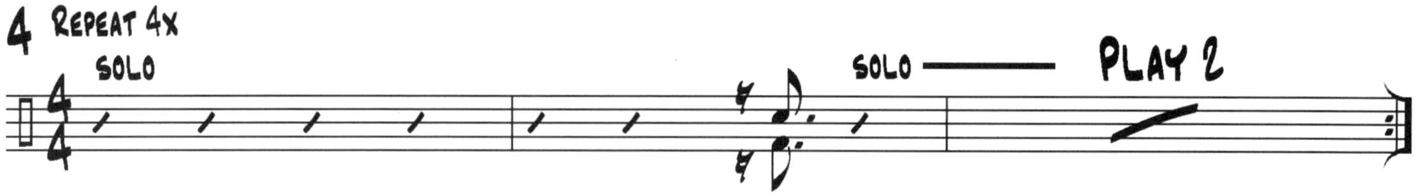
4 Repeat 4x
SOLO
SOLO
Play 2

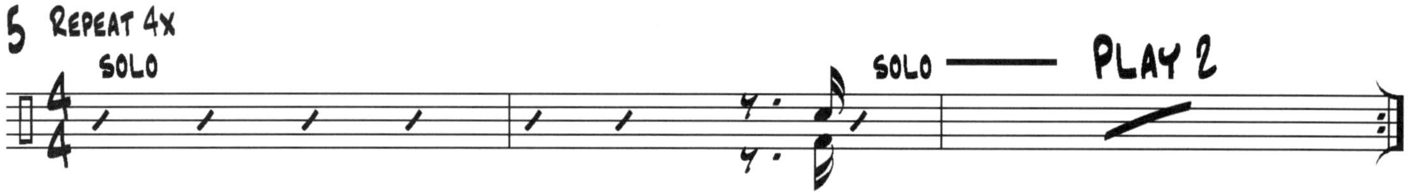
5 Repeat 4x
SOLO
SOLO
Play 2

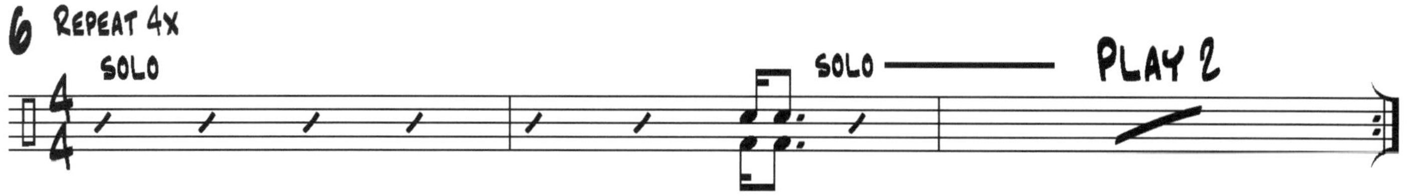
6 Repeat 4x
SOLO
SOLO
Play 2

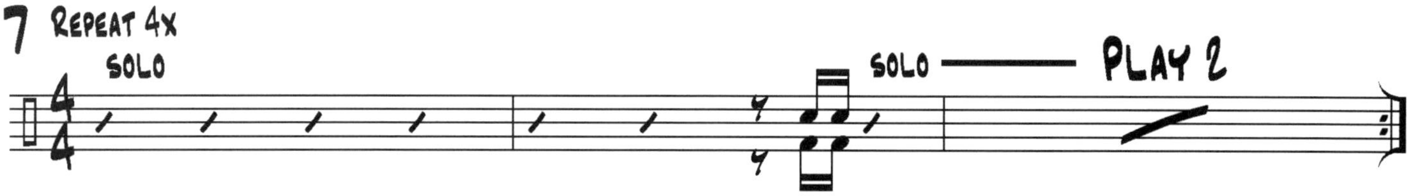
7 Repeat 4x
SOLO
SOLO
Play 2

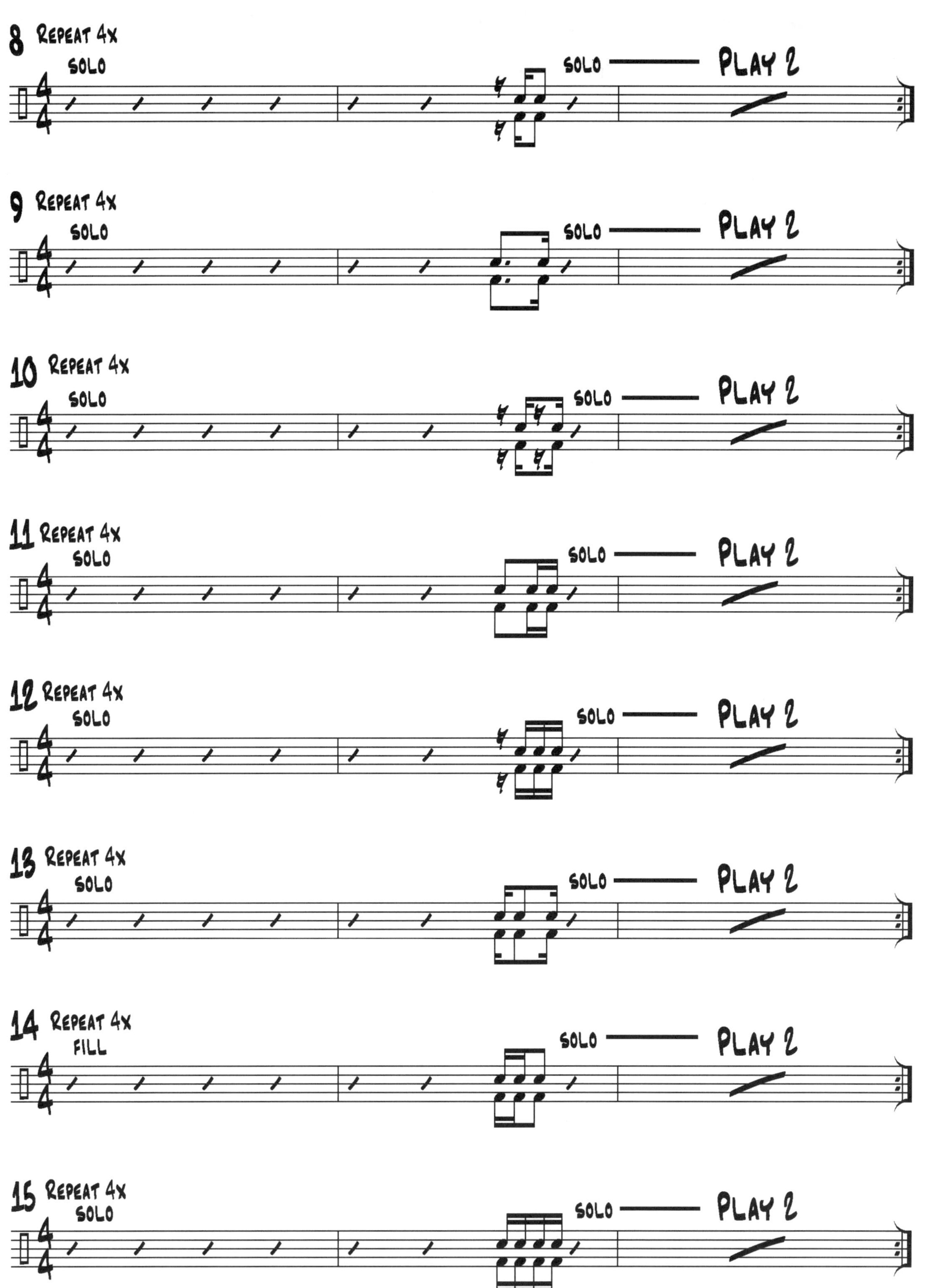
8 REPEAT 4x
SOLO
SOLO
PLAY 2

9 REPEAT 4x
SOLO
SOLO
PLAY 2

10 REPEAT 4x
SOLO
SOLO
PLAY 2

11 REPEAT 4x
SOLO
SOLO
PLAY 2

12 REPEAT 4x
SOLO
SOLO
PLAY 2

13 REPEAT 4x
SOLO
SOLO
PLAY 2

14 REPEAT 4x
FILL
SOLO
PLAY 2

15 REPEAT 4x
SOLO
SOLO
PLAY 2

CD Track 22 96 bpm

CD Track 23 130 bpm

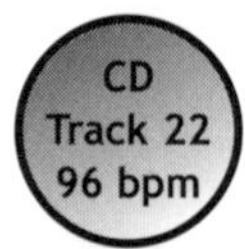

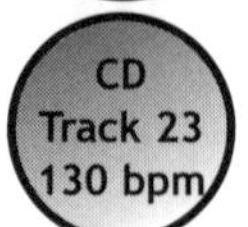

7d. Ensemble Playing 2:

16th-Note Element Ensemble Hits on Beat 4

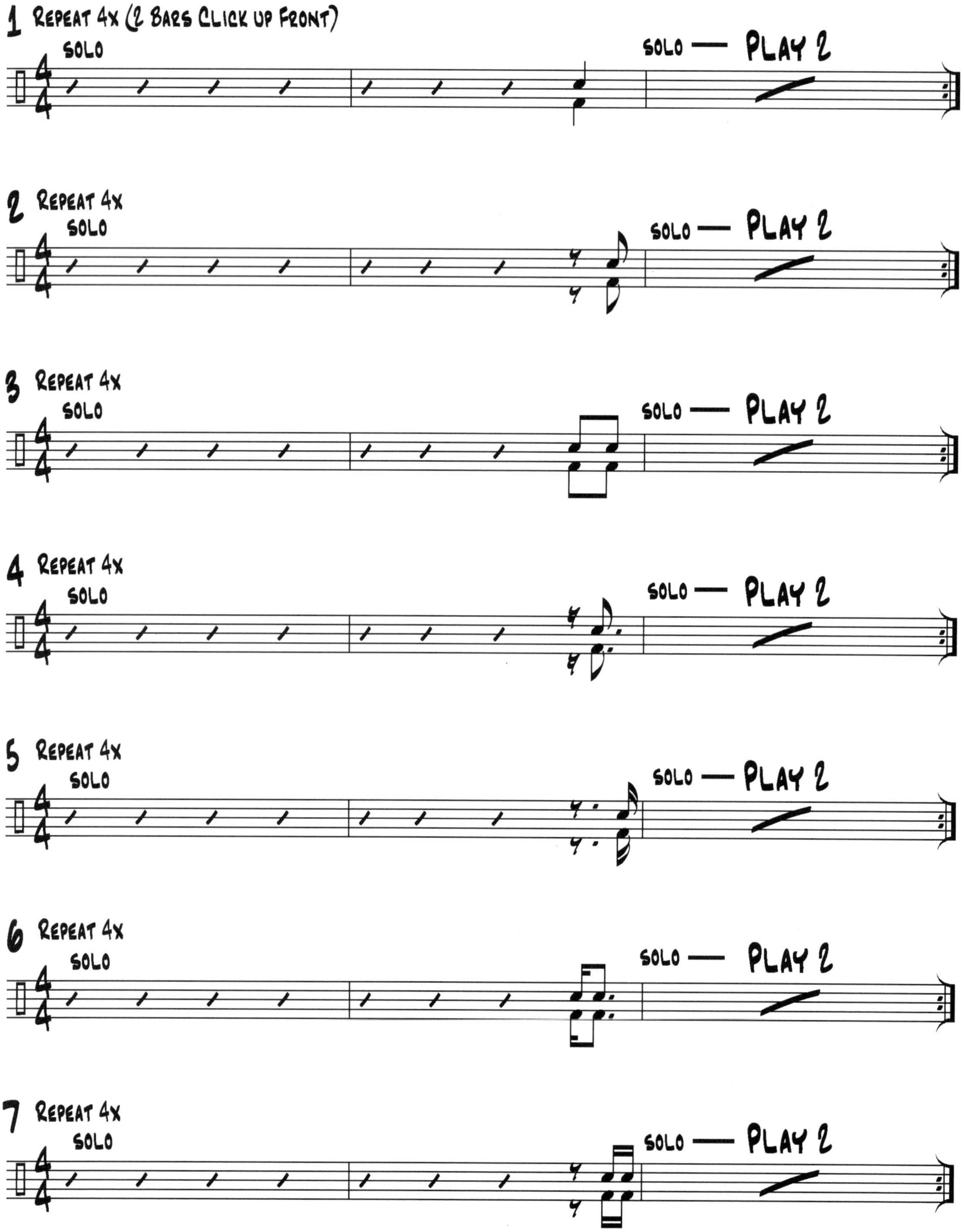
1 Repeat 4x (2 Bars Click up Front)
SOLO
SOLO — PLAY 2
2 Repeat 4x
SOLO
SOLO — PLAY 2
3 Repeat 4x
SOLO
SOLO — PLAY 2
4 Repeat 4x
SOLO
SOLO — PLAY 2
5 Repeat 4x
SOLO
SOLO — PLAY 2
6 Repeat 4x
SOLO
SOLO — PLAY 2
7 Repeat 4x
SOLO
SOLO — PLAY 2

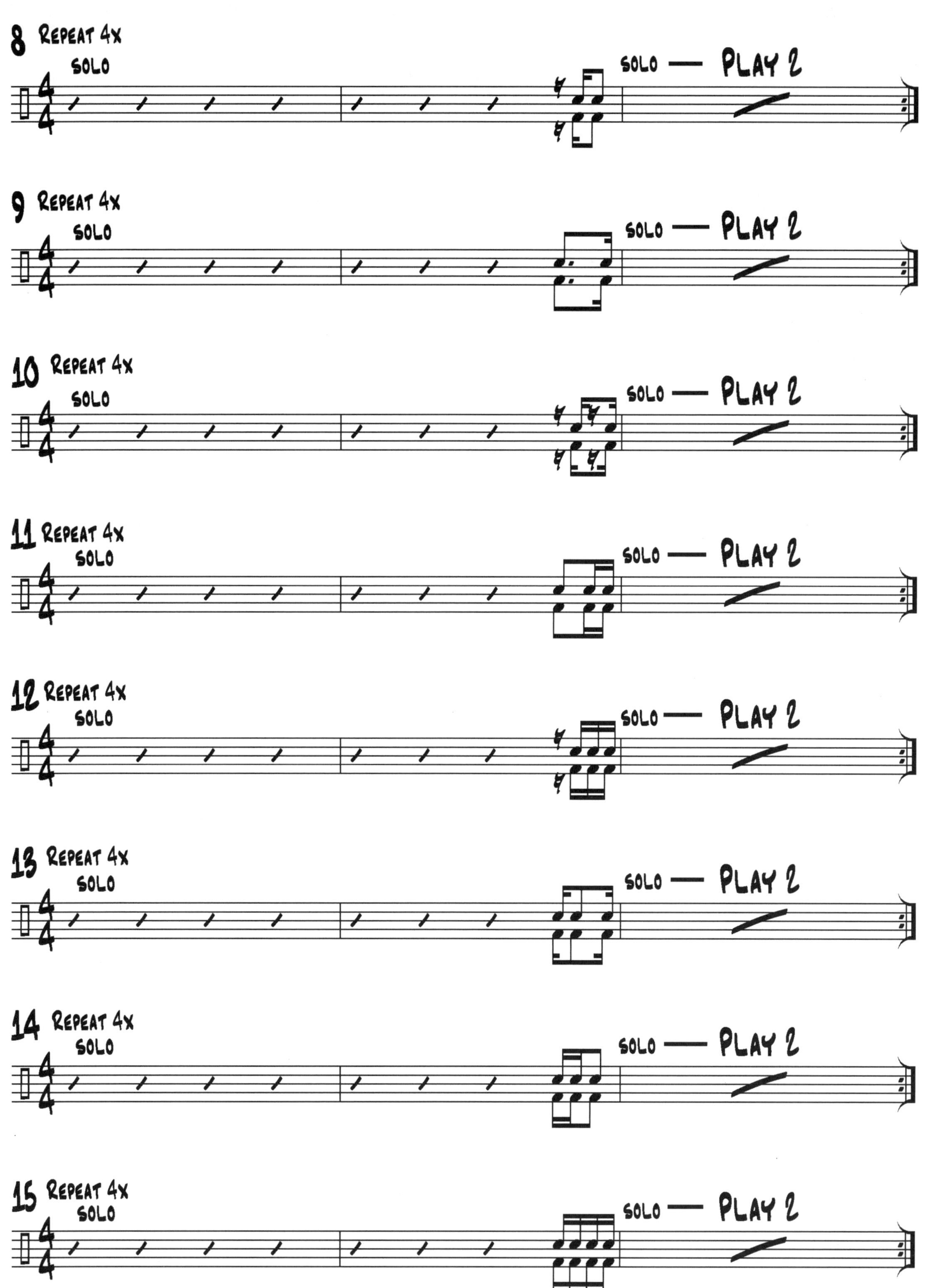
K Ca Sc Ti V Cr Mn Fe Co Ni Cu Kr
8 REPEAT 4x
SOLO
SOLO — PLAY 2
9 REPEAT 4x
SOLO
SOLO — PLAY 2
10 REPEAT 4x
SOLO
SOLO — PLAY 2
11 REPEAT 4x
SOLO
SOLO — PLAY 2
12 REPEAT 4x
SOLO
SOLO — PLAY 2
13 REPEAT 4x
SOLO
SOLO — PLAY 2
14 REPEAT 4x
SOLO
SOLO — PLAY 2
15 REPEAT 4x
SOLO
SOLO — PLAY 2

PART 2:
16th-NOTE ELEMENT GROOVE OSTINATOS

"Press on. Nothing in the world can take the place of persistence."
- Ray A. Kroc

"It is better to be criticized by a wise man then praised by a fool."
- Proverbs

CD Track 24

1. 16th-Note Elements on the Bass Drum

In the groove ostinatos section, you will be using the Elements to improve coordination. With this first set of Groove Ostinatos, we will be working on bass drum independence. The exercises below show a basic rock groove with all the 16th-note Elements played for one measure on the bass drum. Start slow, and use a metronome.

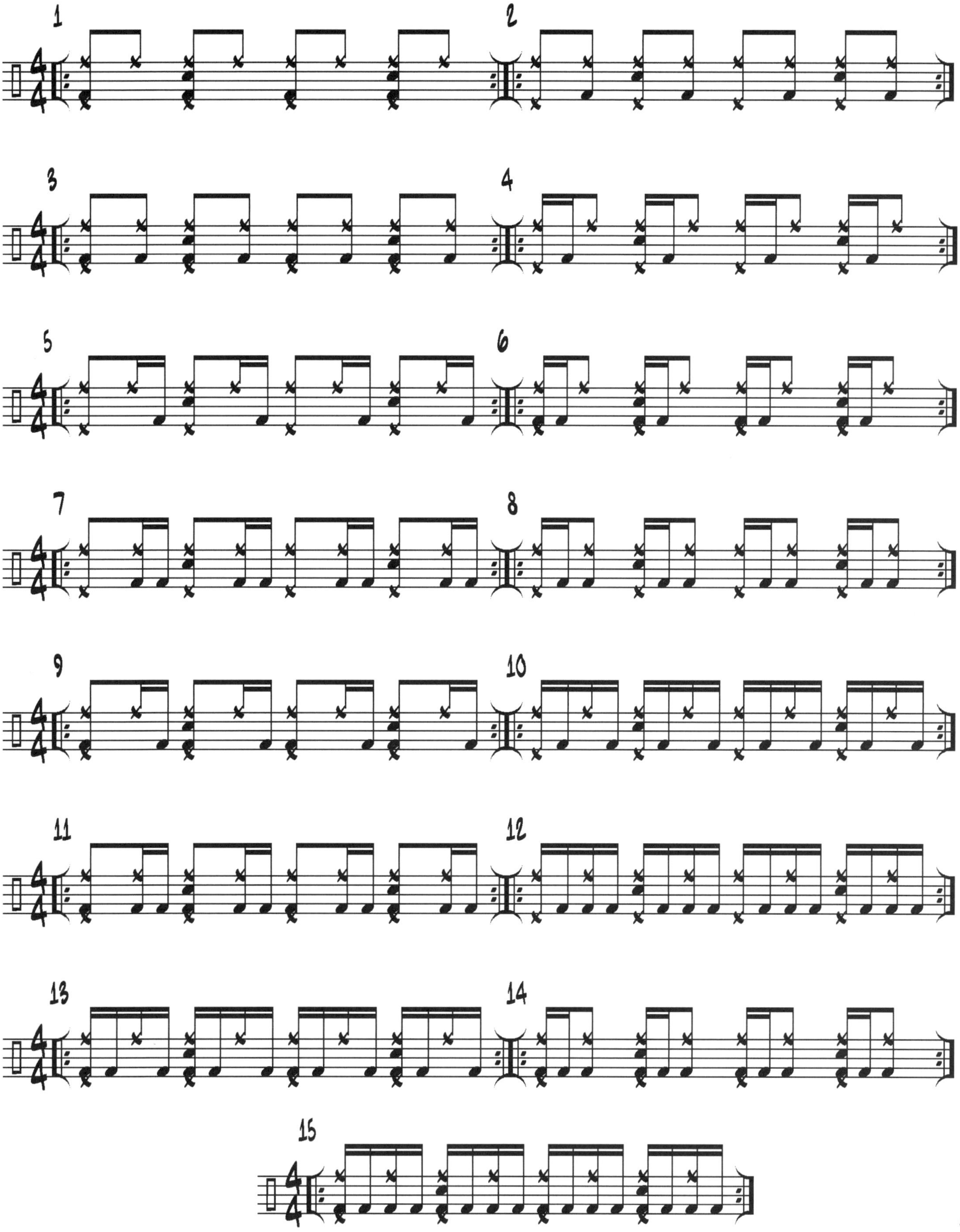

2. 16th-Note Element Basic Groove Ostinatos

This chapter will use the Elements to improve your groove vocabulary and four-way coordination. Learn the following three-limb ostinatos (right hand on ride cymbal, left hand on snare drum, and left foot on hi-hat), then turn to pages 56-57 and practice the variations presented on those pages against these ostinatos on the snare drum.

For further practice material of this kind, refer to *The New Breed* by Gary Chester.

On the CD, John demonstrates a real-world example of grooves created in this manner. Track 25 on the CD is an excerpt from "The Gauntlet" (a tune from John's *Dharma* CD), which shows John using various 16th-note Elements on the bass drum.

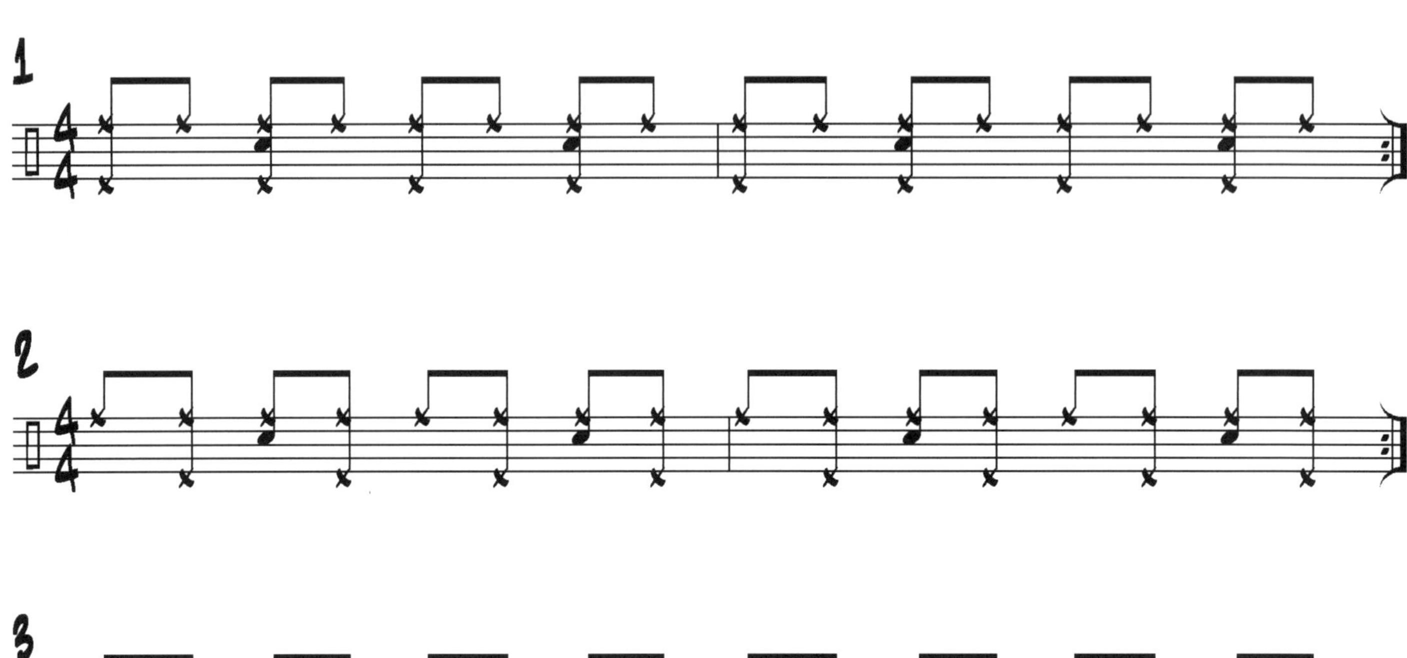

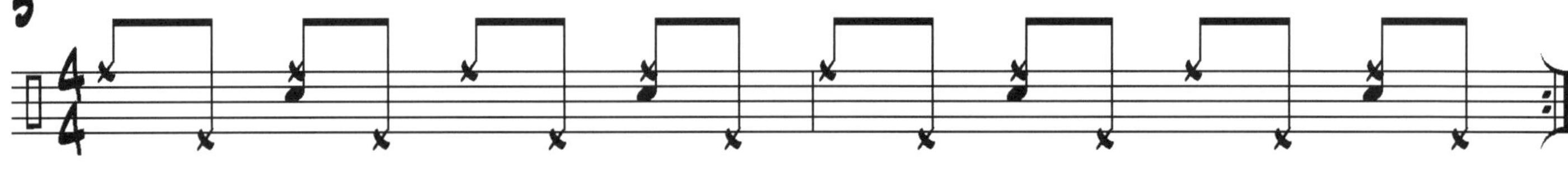

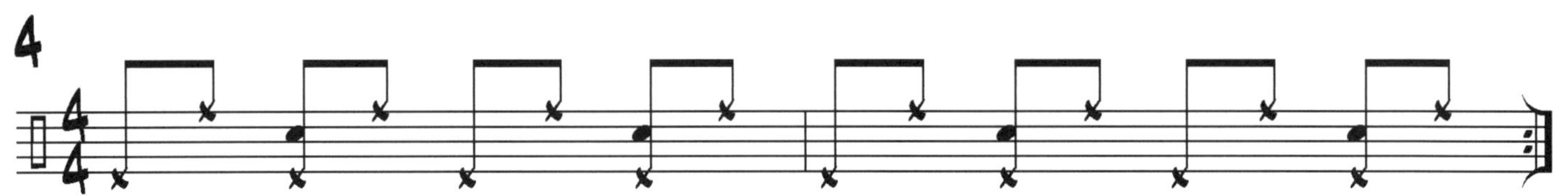

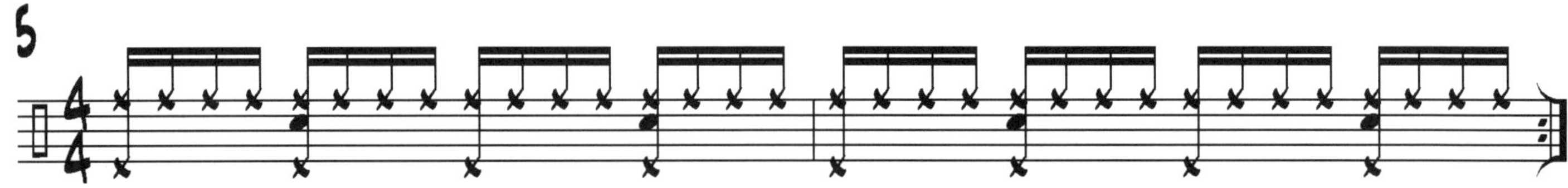

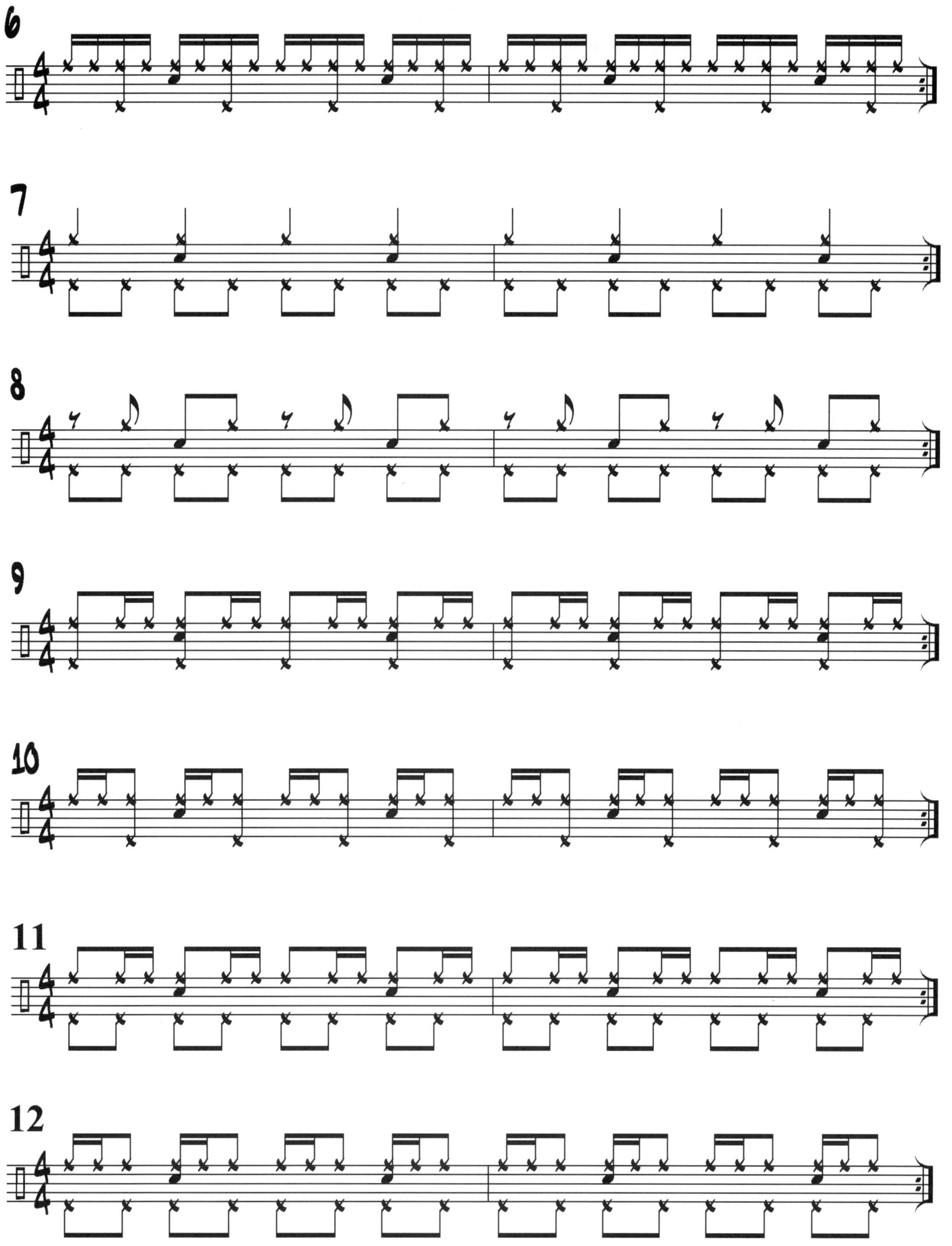

3. 16th-Note Element Advanced Groove Ostinatos

The following examples switch the voice playing the variations to the snare drum. Learn the following three-limb ostinatos (right hand on ride cymbal, left hand on snare drum, and right foot on bass drum), then turn to pages 56-57 and practice the variations presented on those pages against these ostinatos on the snare drum.

For further practice material of this kind, refer to *The New Breed* by Gary Chester.

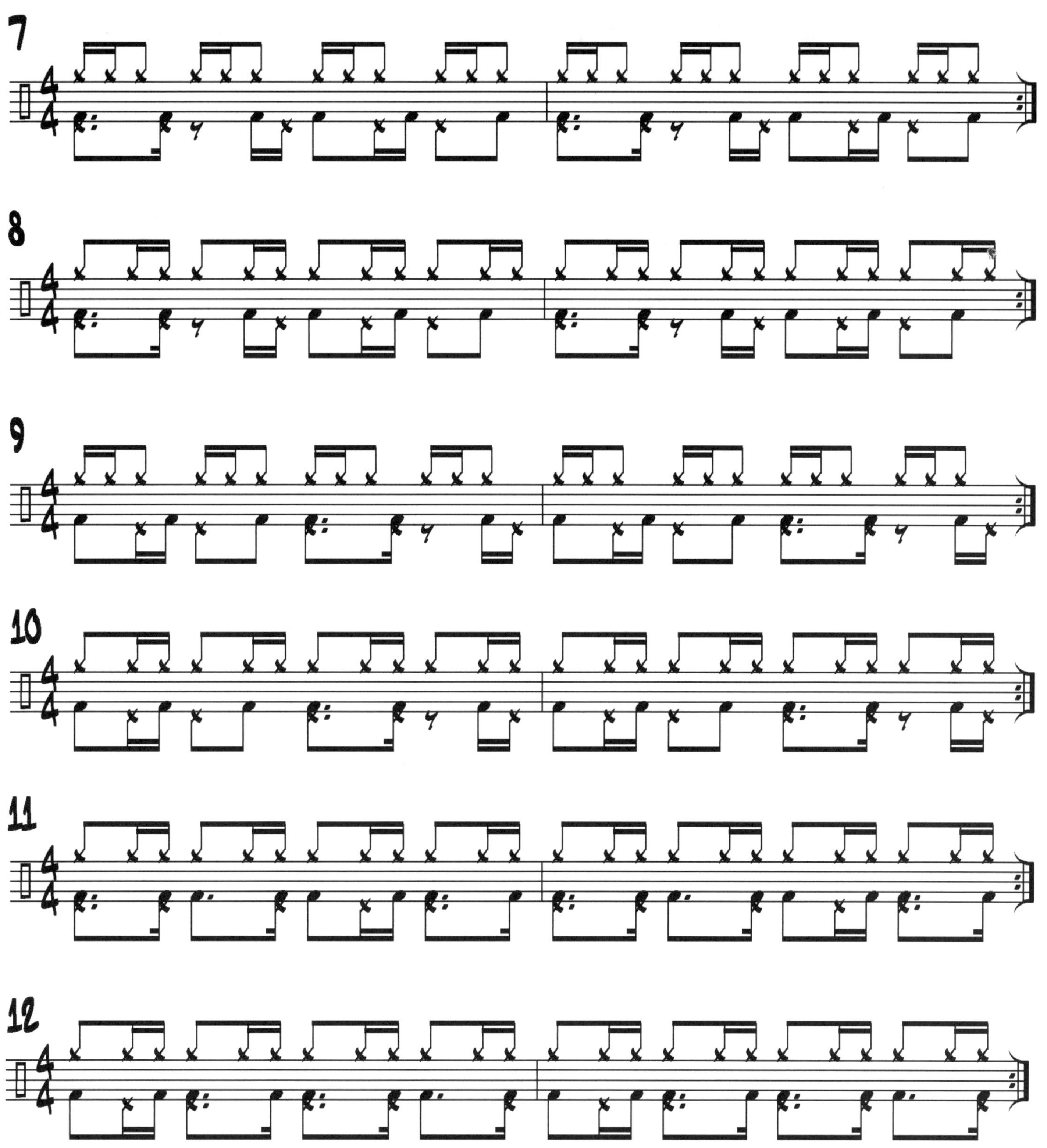

7
8
9
10
11
12

Reading Variations for Sections 2 and 3

These rhythms are to be played with the groove ostinatos presented in parts 2 and 3. In part 2, the bass drum will play these rhythms against the three-limb ostinato, and in part 3, the snare drum will play these rhythms.

Clinic at Drummers Collective, New York City, USA

PART 3:
TRIPLET ELEMENTS

"Use all your facilities but remain detached from them. Facilities are the fruit of your actions and should be used with a big heart. Whilst using all facilities pay attention not to let your spiritual endeavour diminish. Use the facilities but do not get under the influence of them. Do not get impressed! Let your spirituality be visible."
- Kenwood Dennard

1. 8th-Note Triplet Elements

Here are the 8th-note triplet Elements. These are all the possible permutations of one beat of triplets. It is important to be 100% proficient in each one of these. These Elements will become the crucial building blocks of your drumming vocabulary. Practice these individually on a pad or snare drum, with a metronome, until they are comfortable.

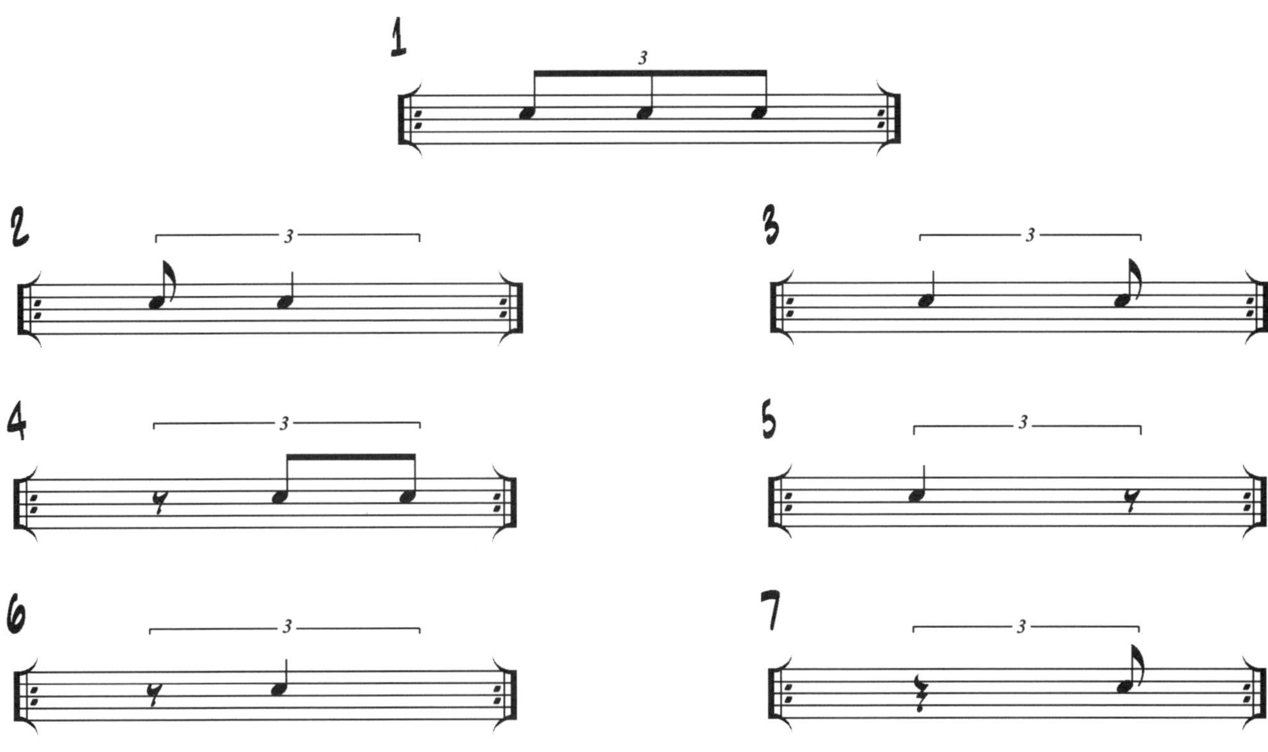

Clinic in Quebec, Canada

1a. Basic Triplet Element Exercise

In the following exercises, practice and repeat each triplet Element on one surface, to make sure you are comfortable. Make sure to count the triplet subdivisions out loud. This is just a practice drill; it doesn't yet have anything to do with applying the Elements with a band.

1b. Accented Elements

For this exercise, play 8th-note triplets as low strokes (2-3" off the drum) and then accent the Elements as full strokes. Dynamic control is key in this exercise; clearly execute the accented Elements.

6

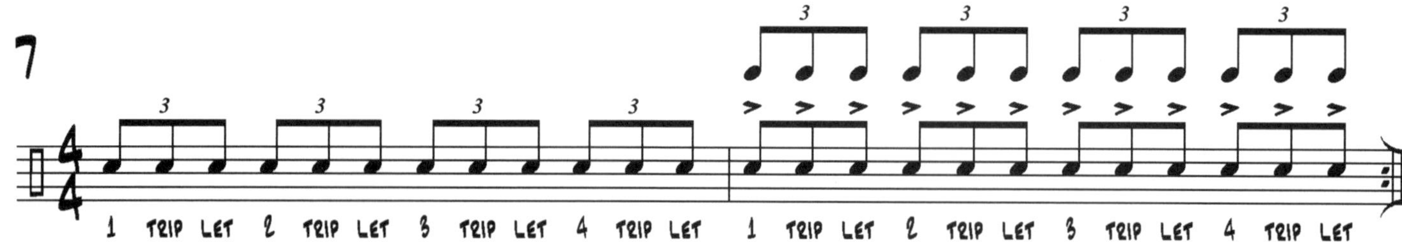

7

Dom Famularo and John, 2002

CD Track 26

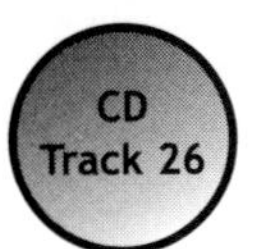

1c. Accented Elements 2

Now try this exercise with accented triplet Elements in a three-bar-phrase flow.

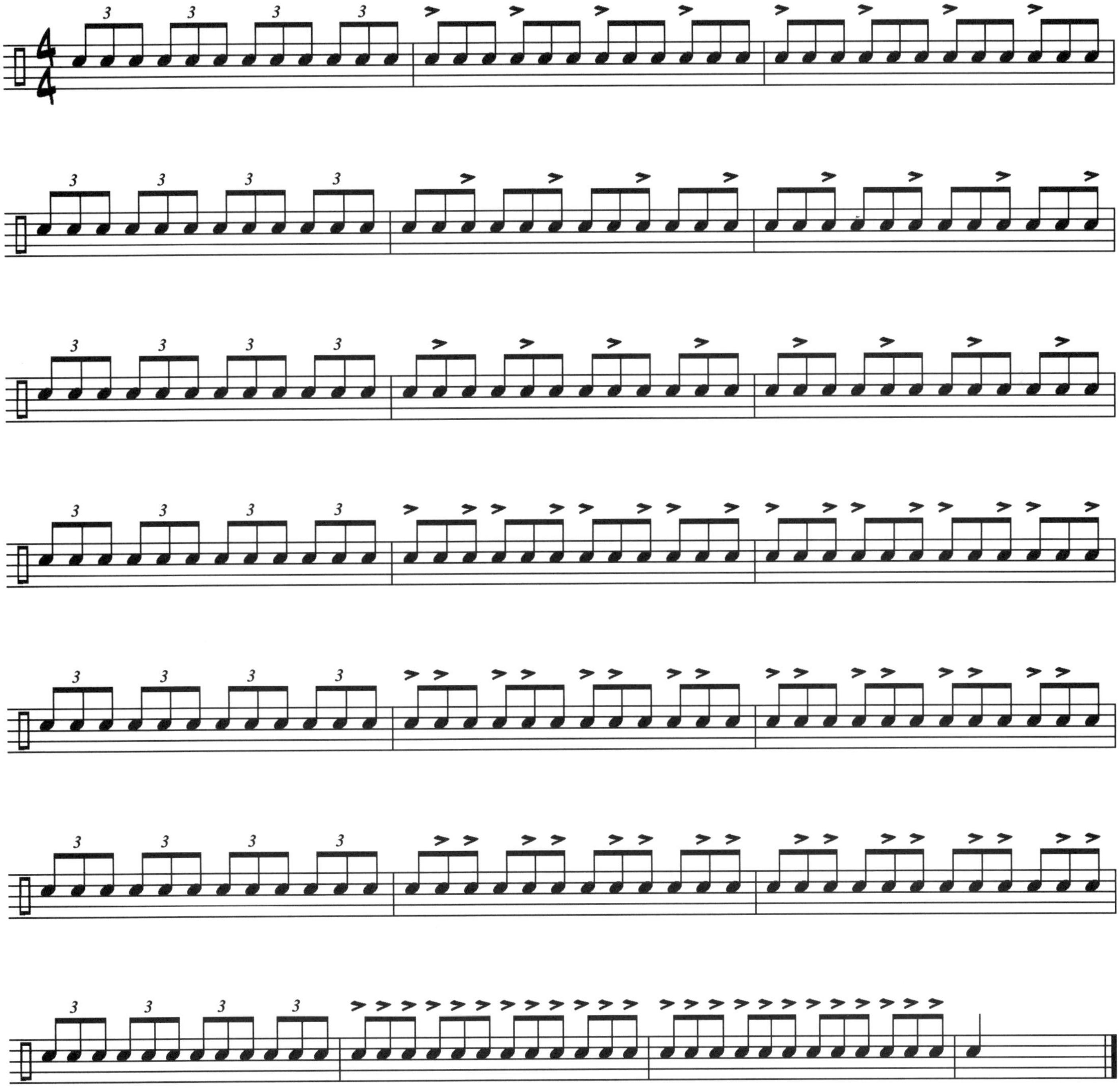

2a. Element Improvisation

The following exercise is an example of Elements improvised as accents in a triplet flow. I improvised these accents while thinking of various Elements and letting them come out naturally. Try to play this exercise with the unaccented notes as low strokes and the Elements (the accents) as full strokes. Make sure to keep a steady flow of low-stroke triplets going.

When you are comfortable with this, improvise your own Elements as accents while playing triplets.

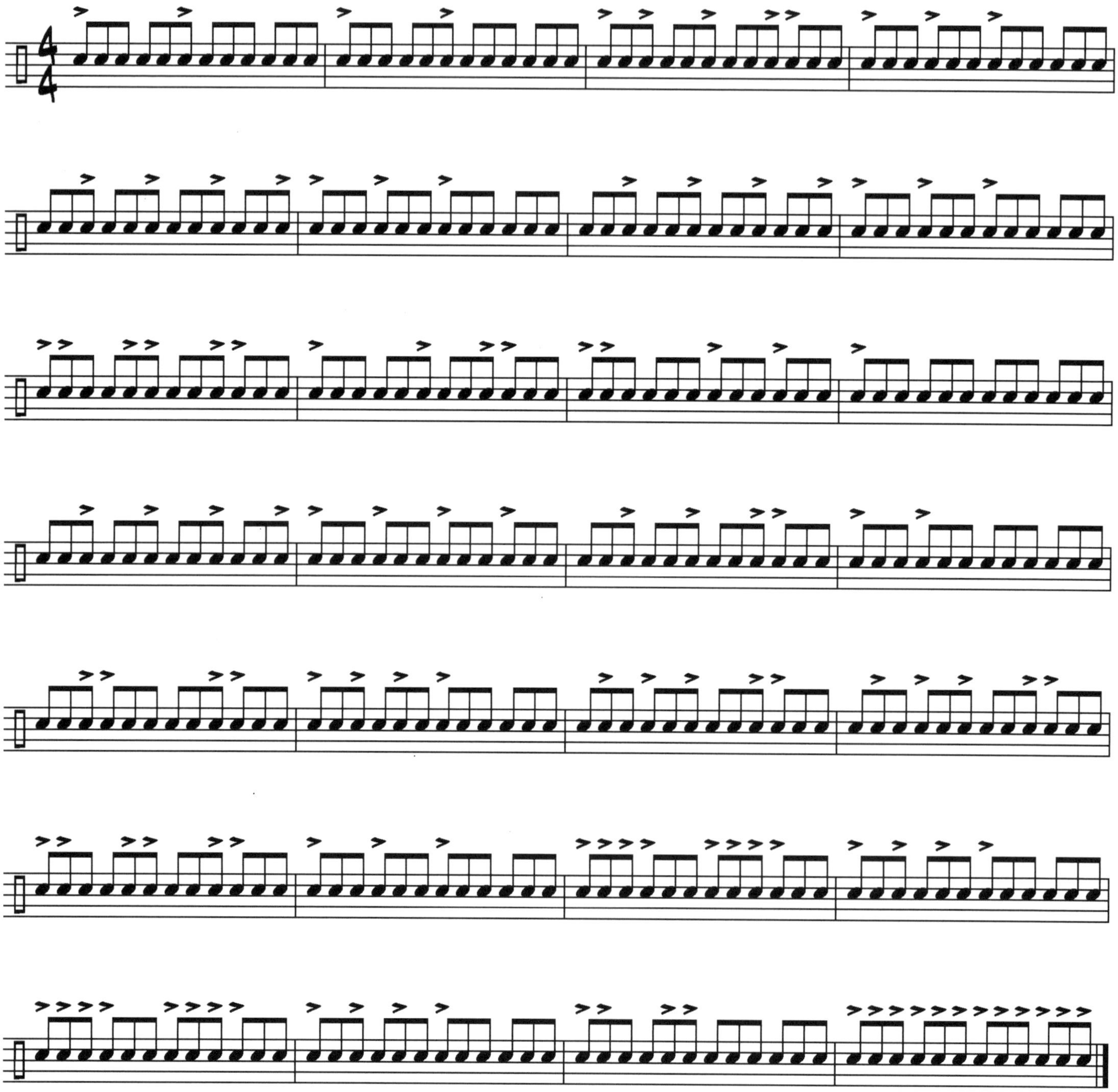

CD Track 28

2b. Element Improvisation

As we did with sixteenths, we'll now improvise around the kit with triplet Elements. Remember to improvise your own ideas, using all the triplet Elements and all the different sound sources on your kit.

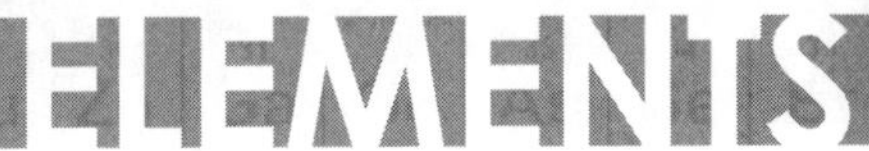

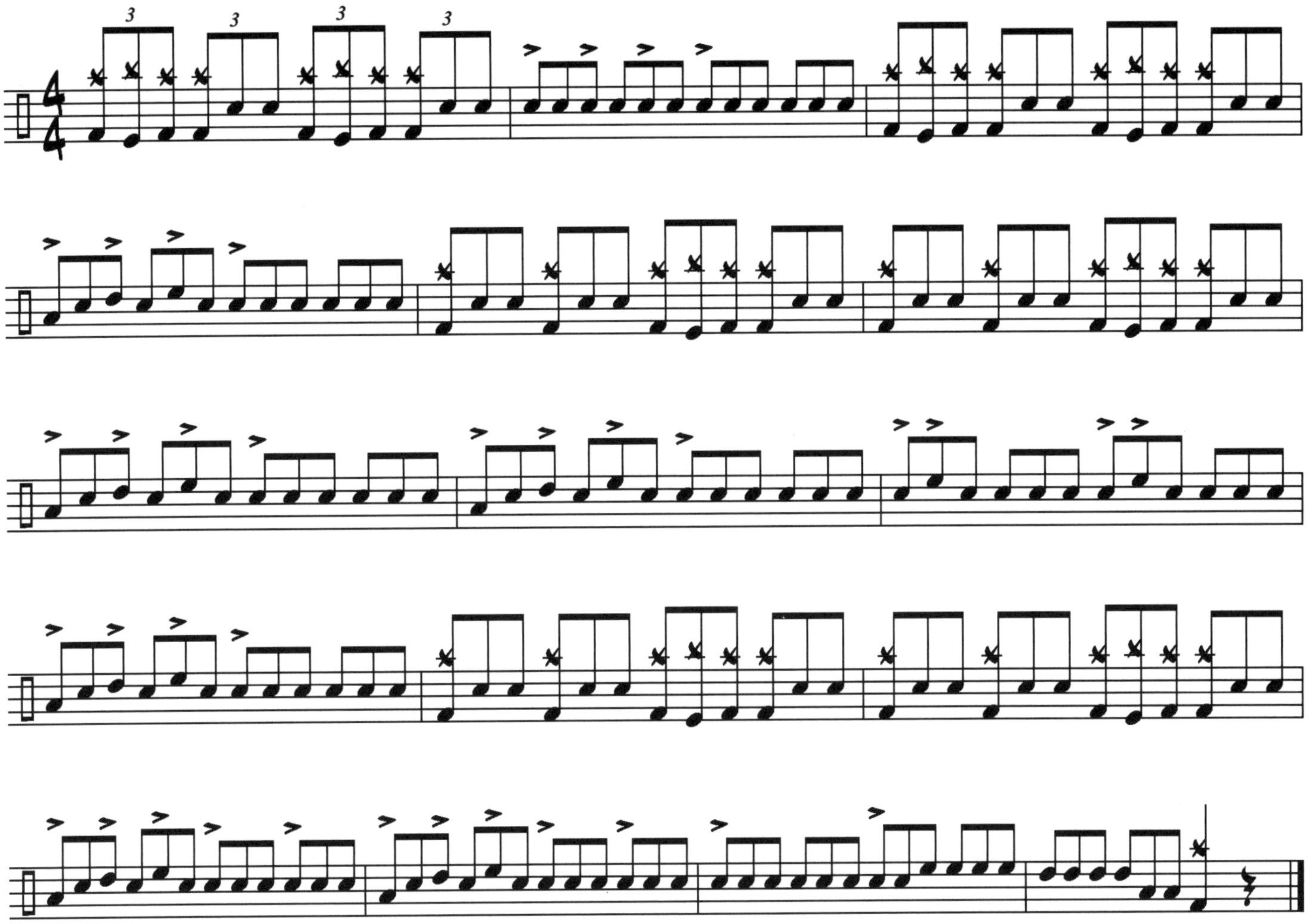

3. Accented Element Triplet Rolls: Intro

This section is similar to section 3 in part 1 of this book, except that this time we will insert accented Elements into a flow of triplet rolls. Play the roll as low strokes (2-3") and the accents as half strokes (6-9"). Be certain that when you accent the notes of the Element, that each accent is a *single* stroke, not a double! The ability to execute clean single-stroke accents while playing a roll in between is very important.

This exercise also helps in counting rolls. Now you can use rolls in your grooves and solos and not get lost!

As written:

As played:

3a. Accented Element Triplet Rolls

For this routine, play an 8th-note triplet even roll and accent each Element. Play the roll as low strokes (2-3") and the accents as half strokes (6-9"). Note: The roll stops for each accent. This exercise helps in counting rolls. Now you can use rolls in your grooves and solos and not get lost!

CD Track 29

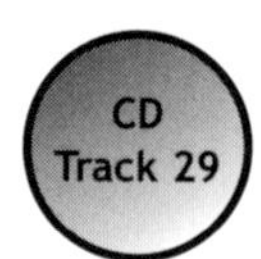

3c. Triplet Roll Element Improvisation

The next step is to play an open triplet roll and then randomly insert Elements as single-stroke accents. First try playing my written example of this, and then improvise your own. Keep your ears open for melodies that the Elements make, and let the melodies guide you as you improvise.

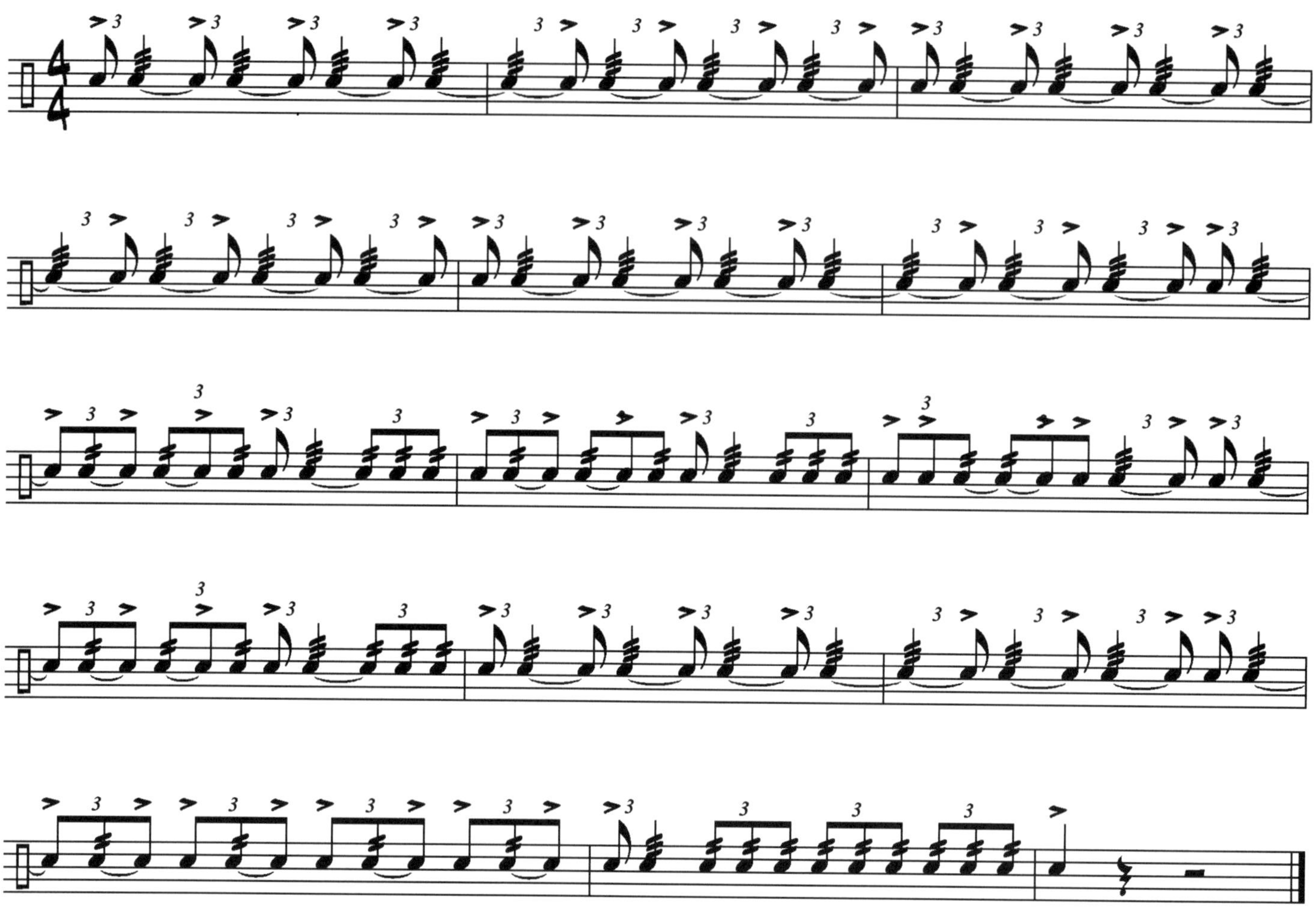

3d. Improvisation with Improvised Voicings

Now let's take our ability to play open triplet rolls with improvised Elements and apply it to the drumset.

First try my improvised example below and check out how I orchestrated Elements all over the kit and kept the roll flow going on my snare drum.

First, play this exercise as written; then improvise your own Elements and orchestrate them on your kit. To do this, you must improvise on two levels: 1) which Elements you are going to accent, and 2) on which part of the drumset you are going to play them. Try to play this exercise for as long as you can without stopping. If you stumble or break the flow, stop and start again from the beginning. Also keep in mind that this is a vocabulary builder. Some of these ideas are going to feel right and some will not. As you play, remember what feels and sounds right. Store these ideas away in your memory to be used again in the future. The ones that don't feel and sound good? Just forget them. Be open to experimenting and letting yourself just play without too much thought.

4. Triplet Element Application:
Three Bars of Time and a One-Bar Fill

In this routine you will play three bars of any triplet-based groove, followed by a one-bar fill. For the fill, think of an Element and orchestrate it on the kit. Your job is to voice the Element in the most musical way possible. Use a metronome so that your fills don't speed up or slow down.

After you play through the entire exercise many times, the next step is to combine Elements when you play fills. If you can make one Element in a fill sound good, then once you start to mix and match all the Elements you will be on your way to making your vocabulary larger and larger.

These examples contain all of the basic triplet Elements, to be used as the basis for your fills.

5. Additional Applications

Random Voicing Exercise 1

Now that you have practiced the Elements with the previously outlined routines, you should spend some time improvising with the Elements.

Take each Element one at a time and voice it around the kit for as long as you can without stopping or repeating yourself. The goal is to be able to play the Element for up to five minutes and keep it musical and interesting. At first you might find yourself falling back on the same ideas over and over again. Push yourself to continue practicing until you can improvise with each Element more freely, without repeating the same orchestrations. Once you can play each Element in this way your vocabulary will be elevated to the next level.

Random Voicing Exercise 2

Count 16th notes out loud and play any Element at random on any voice. This will help to develop your inner clock as well as further your ability to improvise orchestrations and placement of the Elements.

6. Triplet Ensemble Playing 1

Now, as we did with the sixteenth Elements, we will practice the triplet Elements as ensemble figures.

This first set of exercises presents all the Elements one at a time, occuring on beat 1 of the bar. The next set moves all the Elements back to beat 2, then beat 3, and beat 4. When you have mastered these exercises, you will easily be able to catch any one-beat triplet-based ensemble hit in any position in the bar.

Each track has two bars of time up front. You will then play one bar of time with a fill leading into an ensemble figure in the second bar. Try playing the hits with two basic interpretations. First, play them with "long" sounds (i.e., a cymbal crash), and then with "short" sounds (i.e., a snare accent or other staccato sound).

All ensemble play-alongs on the CD are repeated 4 times.

CD Track 31 110 bpm

CD Track 32 132 bpm

6a. Triplet Ensemble Playing 1:

Triplet Element Ensemble Hits on Beat 1

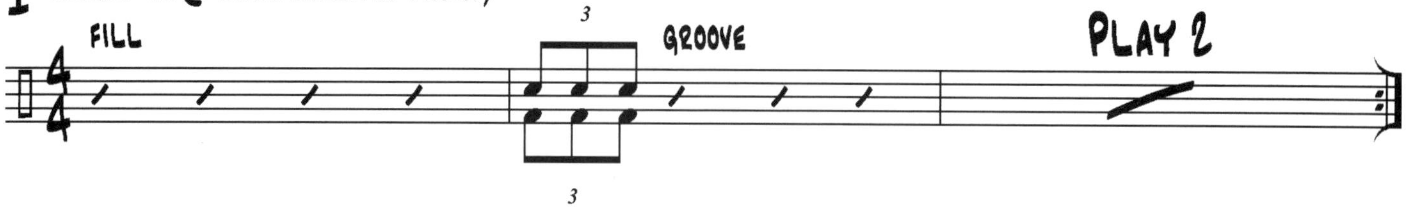

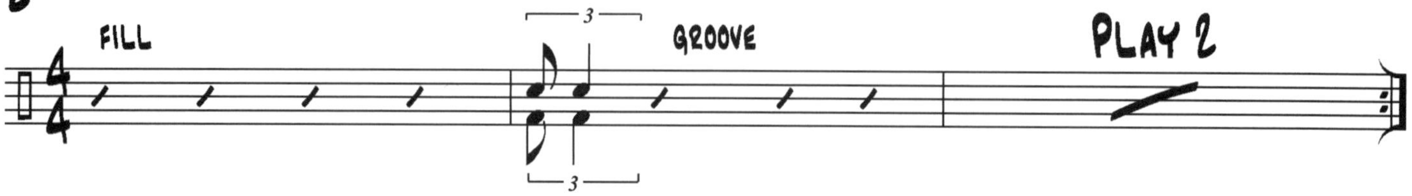

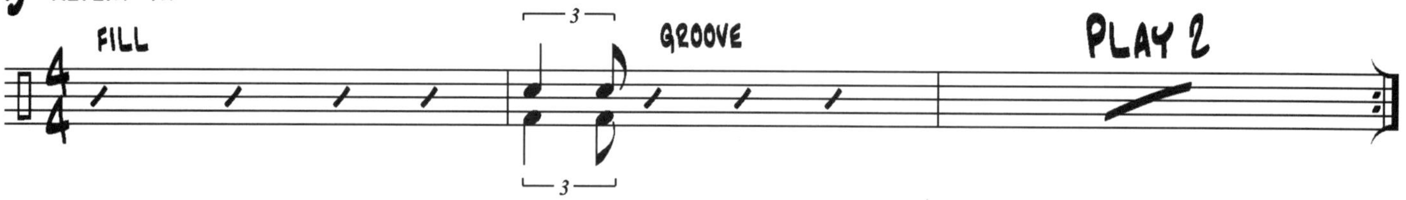

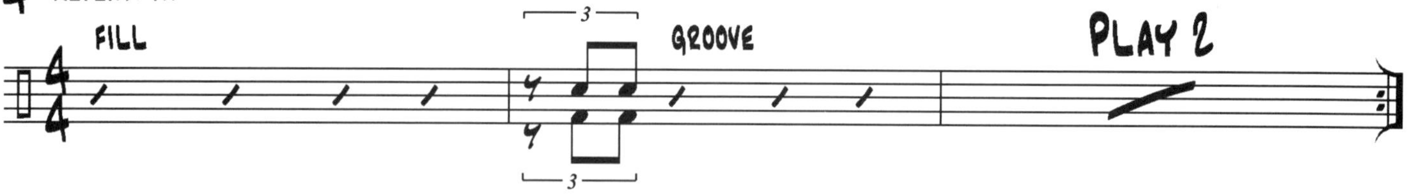

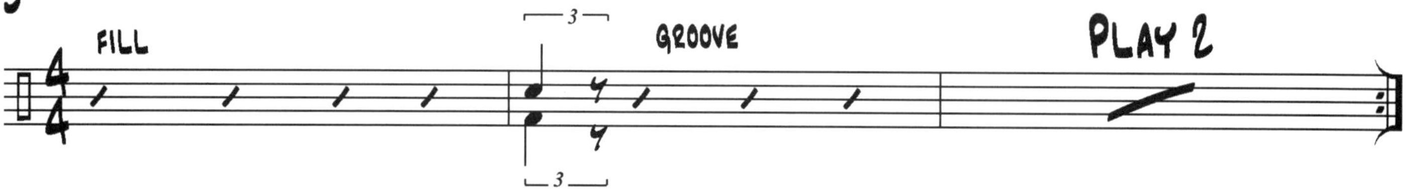

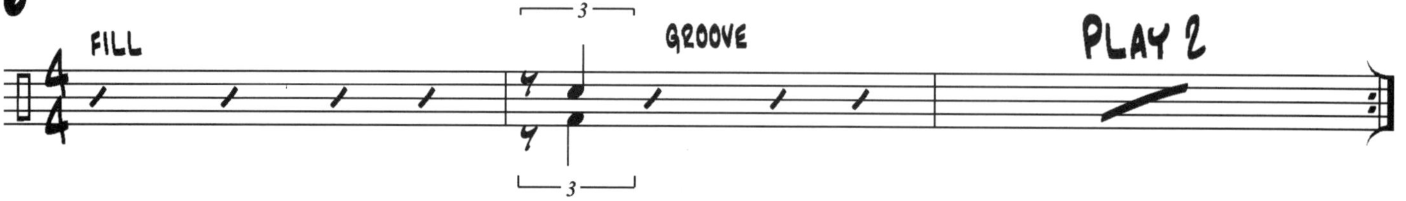

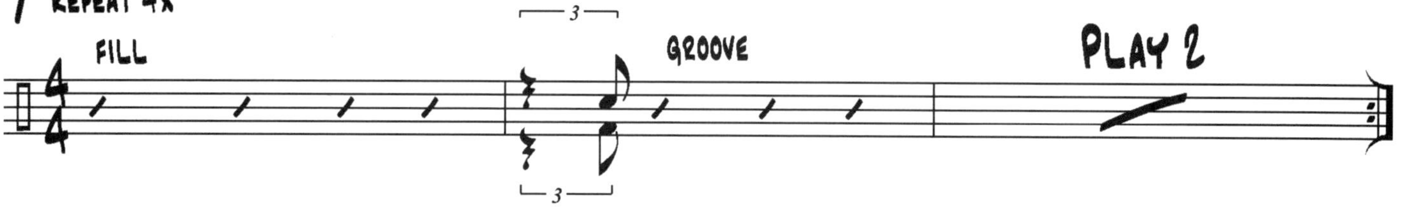

CD Track 33 110 bpm

CD Track 34 132 bpm

6b. Triplet Ensemble Playing 1:

Triplet Element Ensemble Hits on Beat 2

1 REPEAT 4X (2 BARS CLICK UP FRONT)

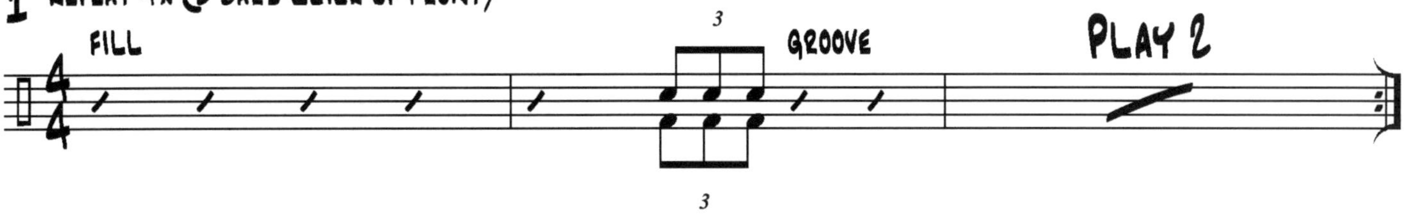

2 REPEAT 4X

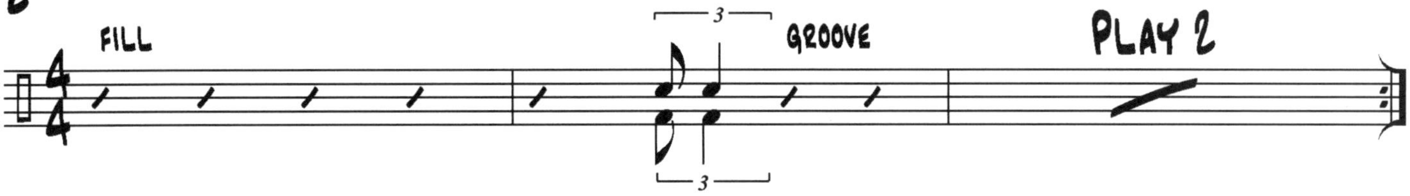

3 REPEAT 4X

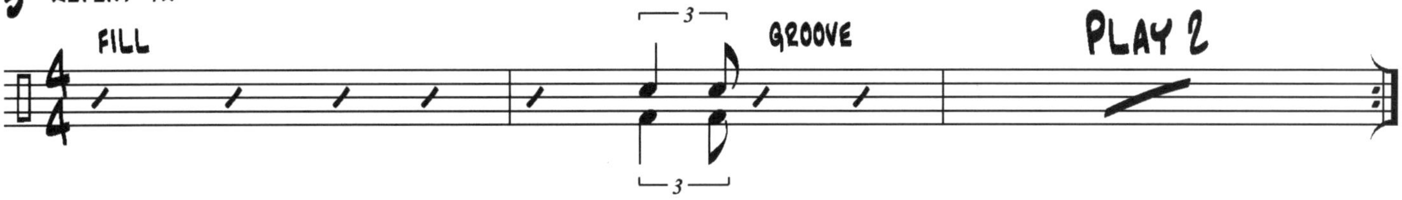

4 REPEAT 4X

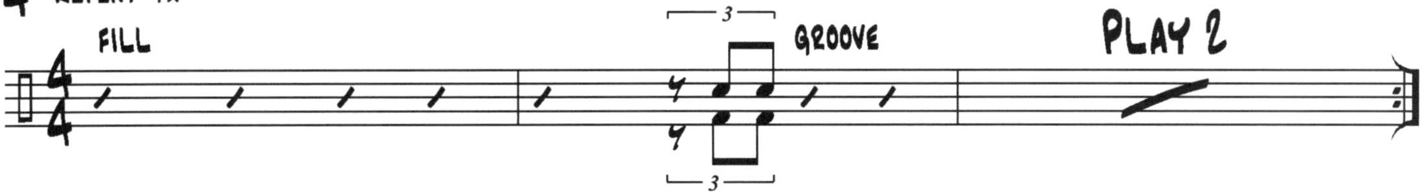

5 REPEAT 4X

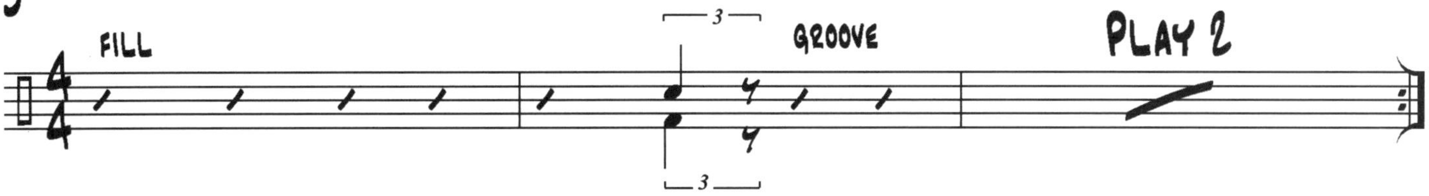

6 REPEAT 4X

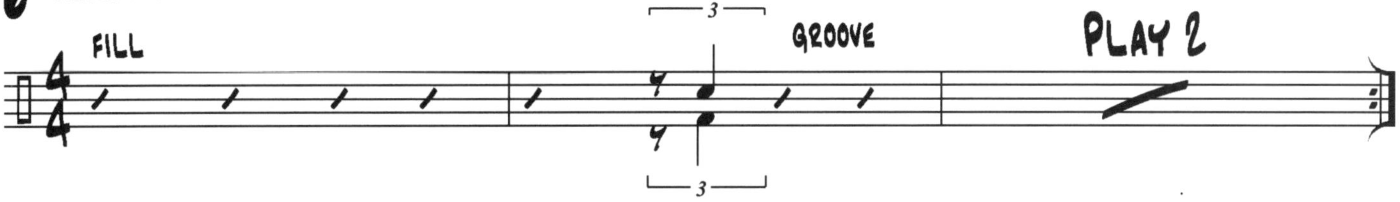

7 REPEAT 4X

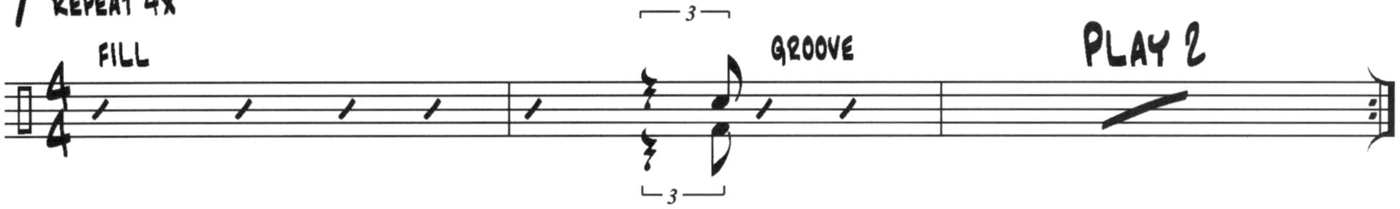

CD Track 35 110 bpm

CD Track 36 132 bpm

6c. Triplet Ensemble Playing 1:

Triplet Element Ensemble Hits on Beat 3

1 REPEAT 4X (2 BARS CLICK UP FRONT)

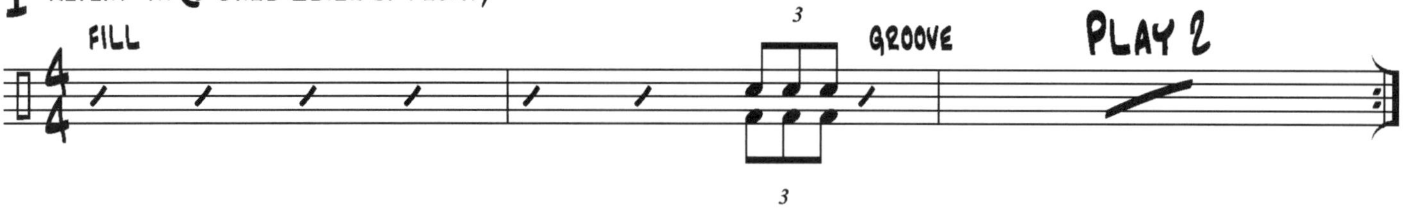
FILL
GROOVE
PLAY 2

2 REPEAT 4X

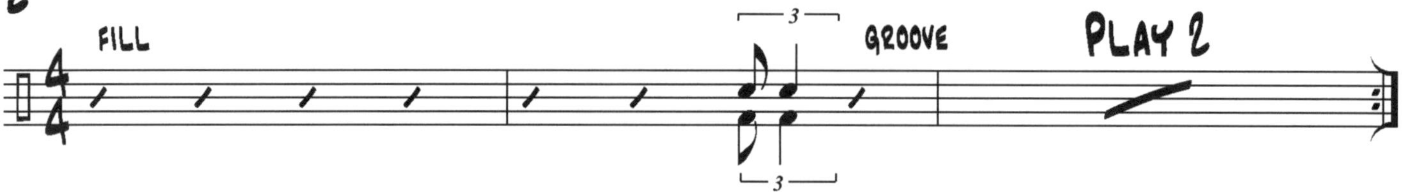
FILL
GROOVE
PLAY 2

3 REPEAT 4X

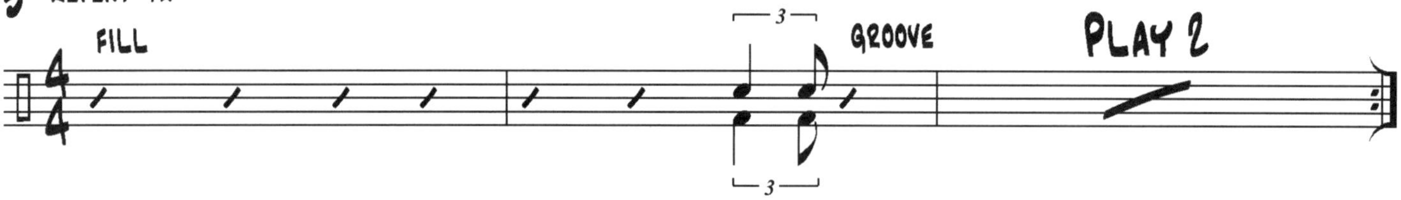
FILL
GROOVE
PLAY 2

4 REPEAT 4X

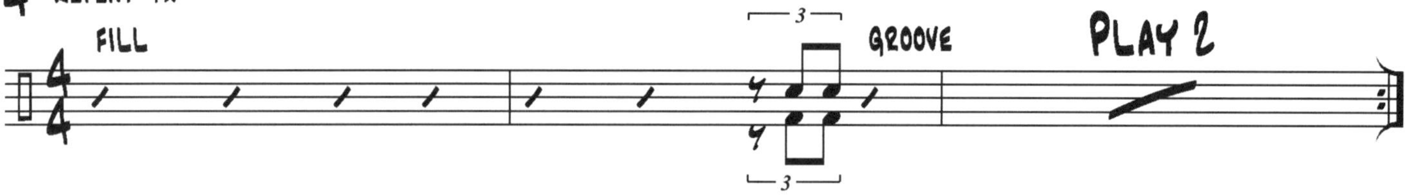
FILL
GROOVE
PLAY 2

5 REPEAT 4X

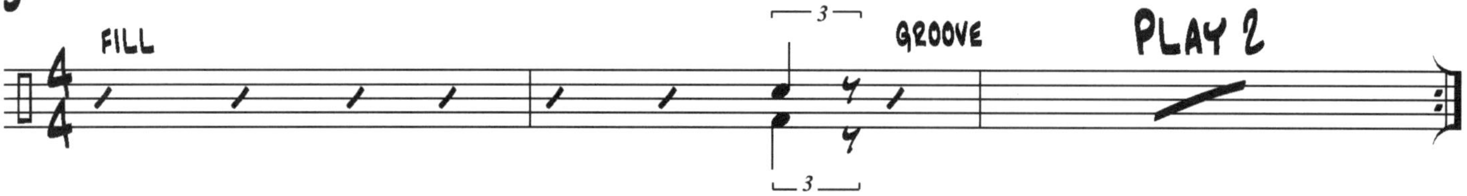
FILL
GROOVE
PLAY 2

6 REPEAT 4X

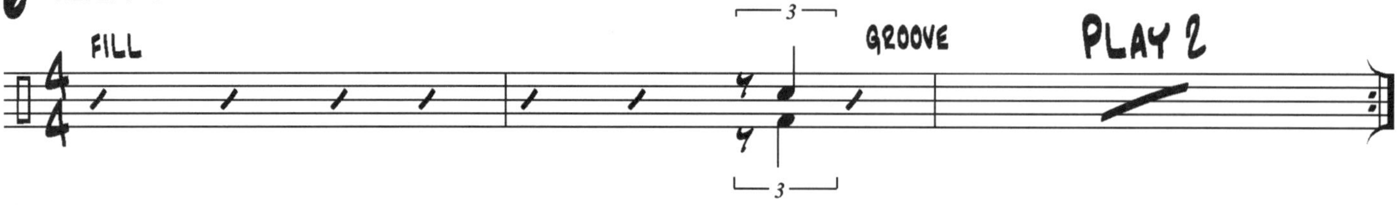
FILL
GROOVE
PLAY 2

7 REPEAT 4X

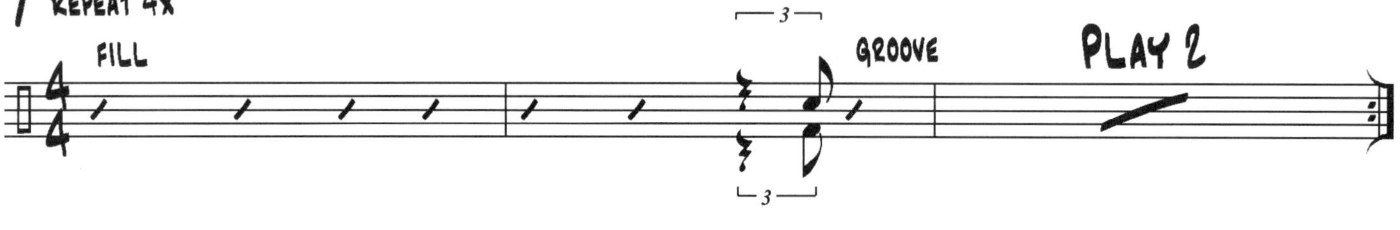
FILL
GROOVE
PLAY 2

CD Track 37 110 bpm

CD Track 38 132 bpm

6d. Triplet Ensemble Playing 1:

Triplet Element Ensemble Hits on Beat 4

1 Repeat 4x (2 Bars Click up Front)

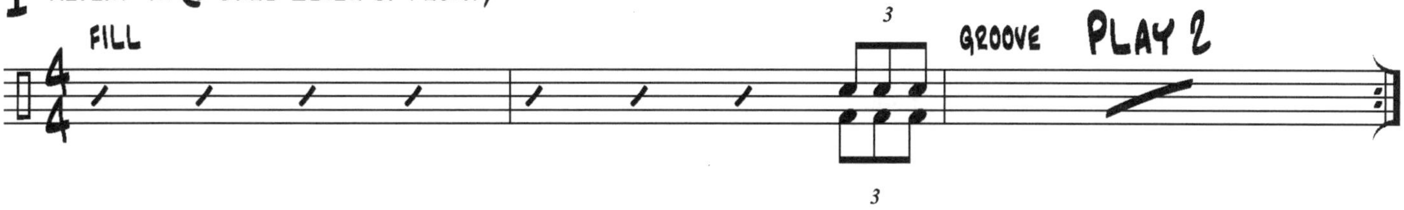

2 Repeat 4x

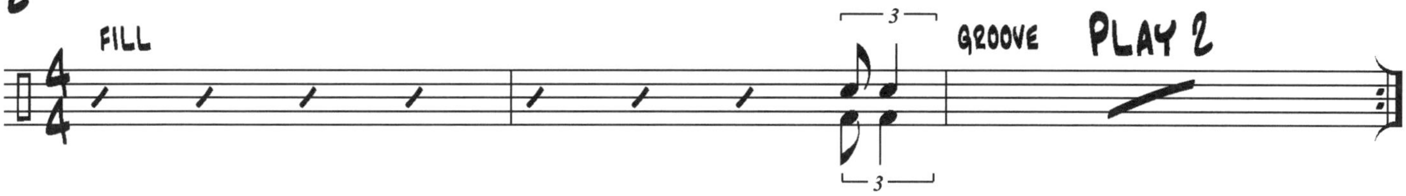

3 Repeat 4x

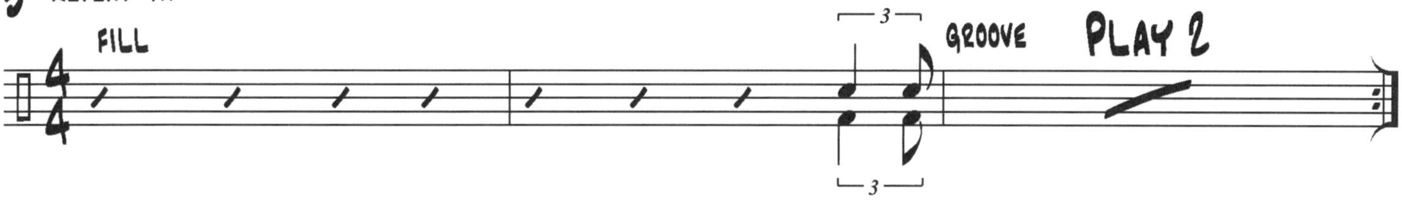

4 Repeat 4x

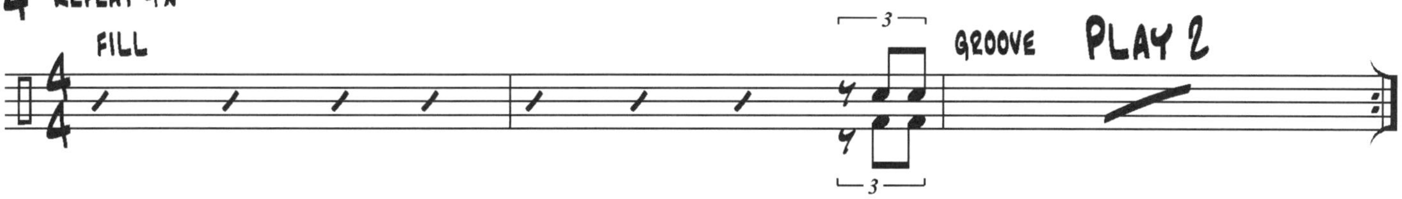

5 Repeat 4x

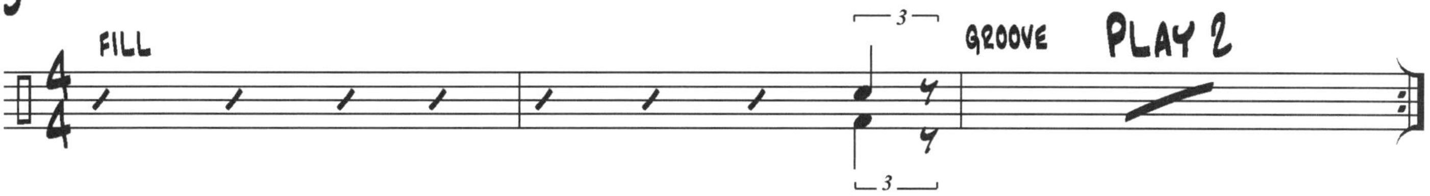

6 Repeat 4x

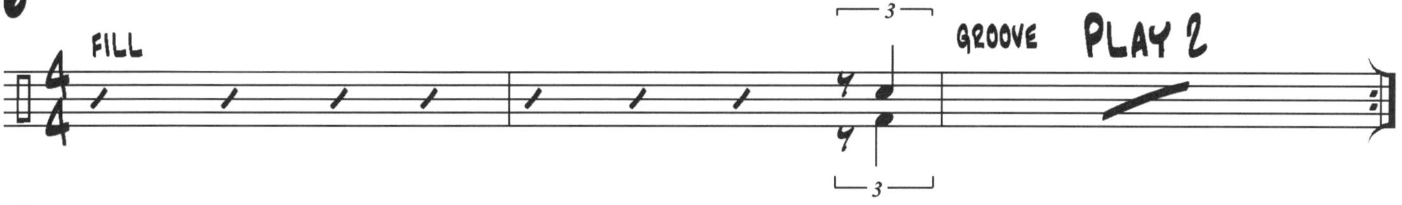

7 Repeat 4x

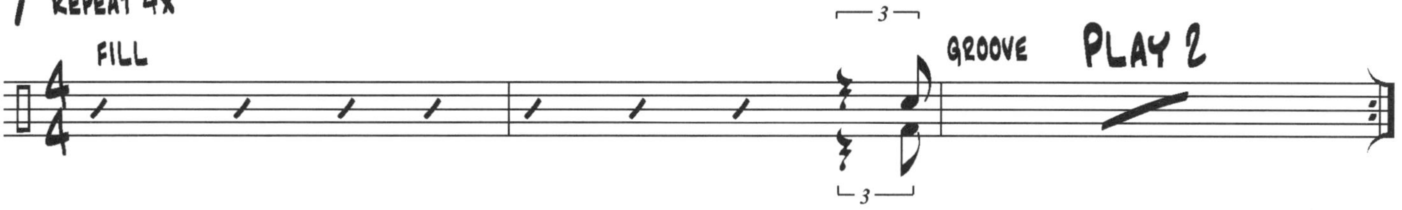

7a. Triplet Ensemble Playing 2:
Triplet Element Ensemble Hits on Beat 1

Now that we have practiced catching the Elements as ensemble figures in the phrase, the next step is to practice soloing around the hits. The Elements in this example are the ensemble hits, and you will be soloing around them in a four-bar phrase. Each track on the CD has two bars of click up front, followed by a four-bar phrase containing an ensemble figure in the second bar. Use these tracks to practice catching the ensemble hits and/or soloing around them. This will ensure that your four-bar phrasing is accurate. Use the accented and roll Elements to give you ideas of solo figures to play around the hits.

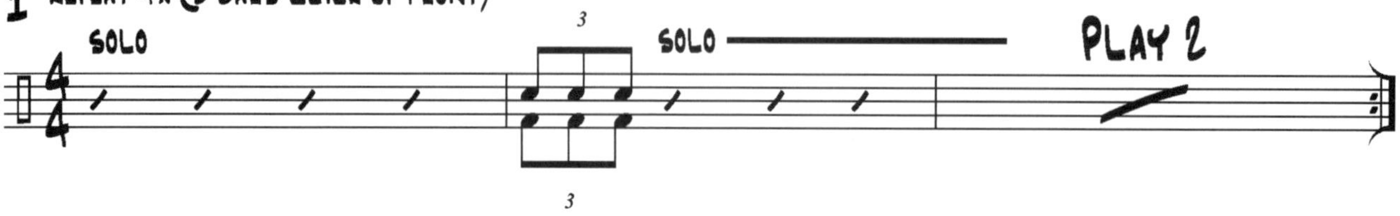

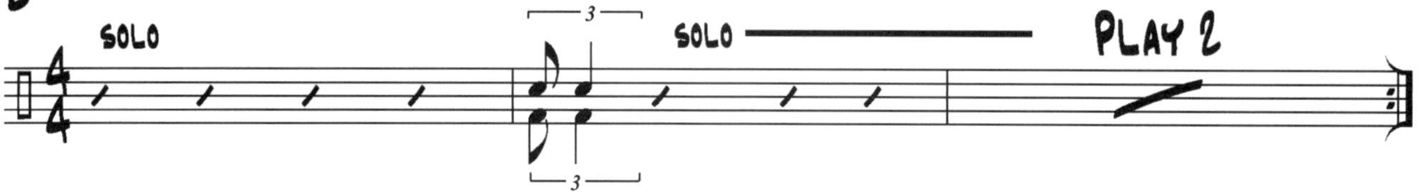

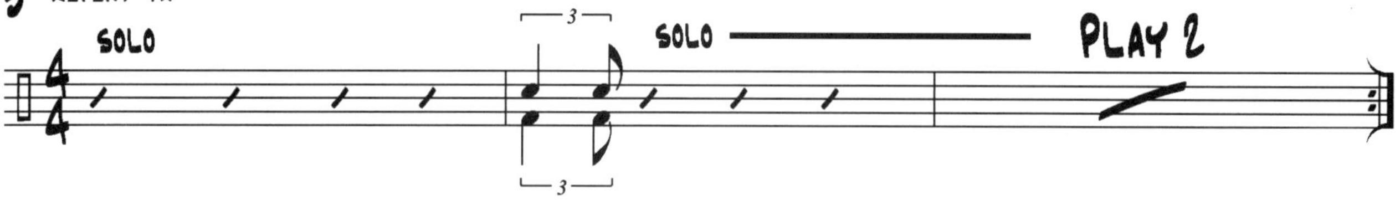

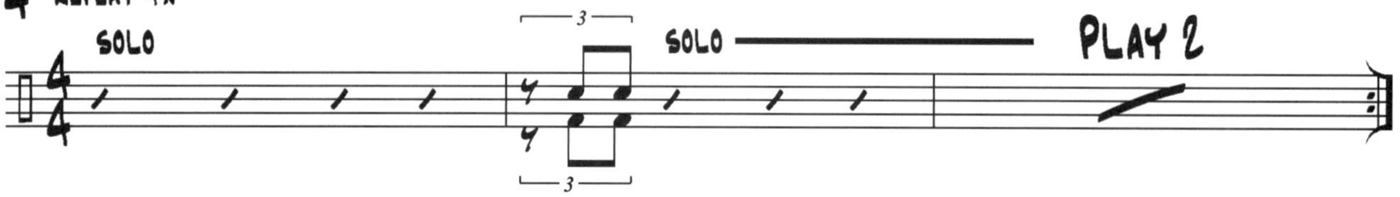

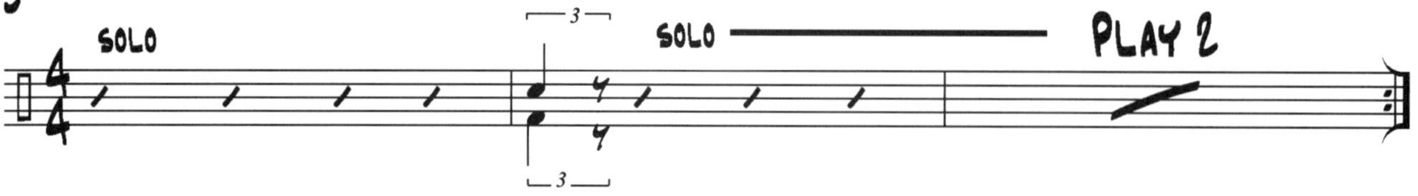

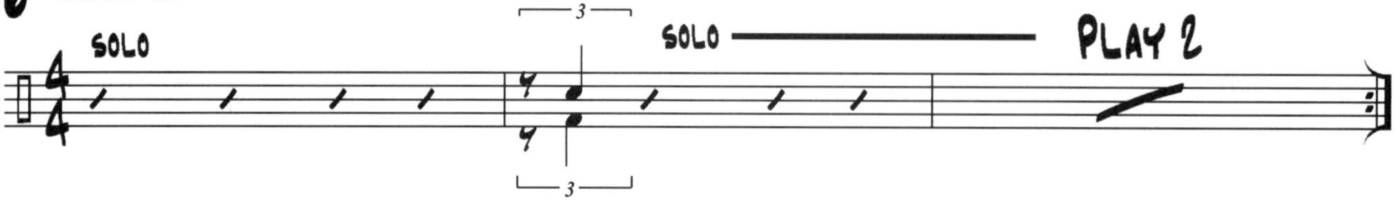

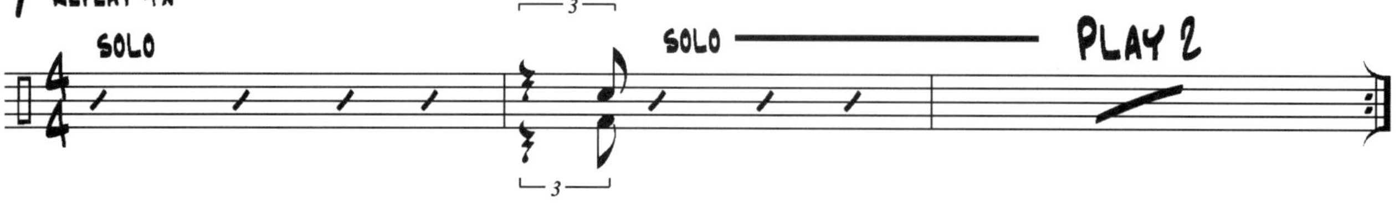

7b. Triplet Ensemble Playing 2:
Triplet Element Ensemble Hits on Beat 2

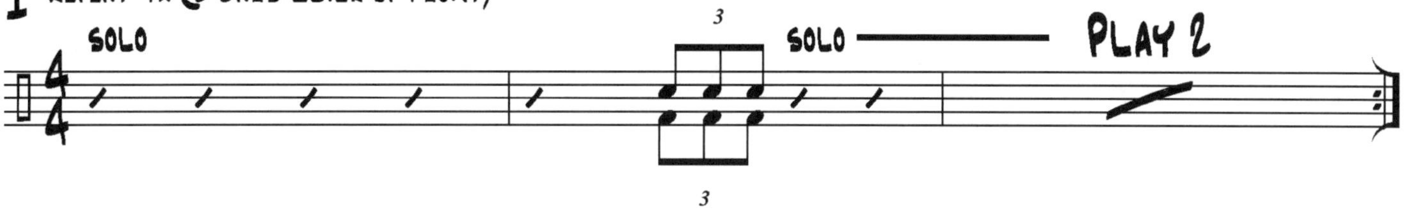

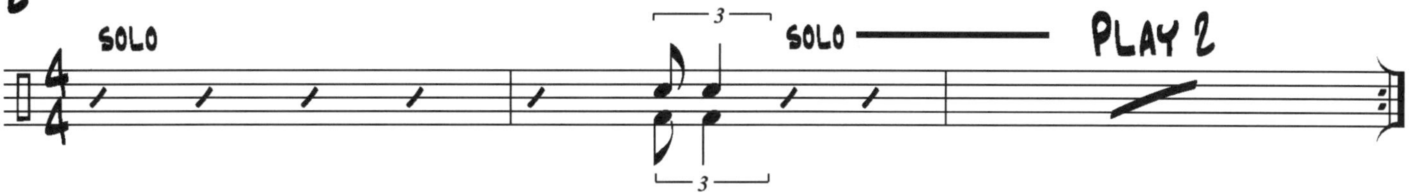

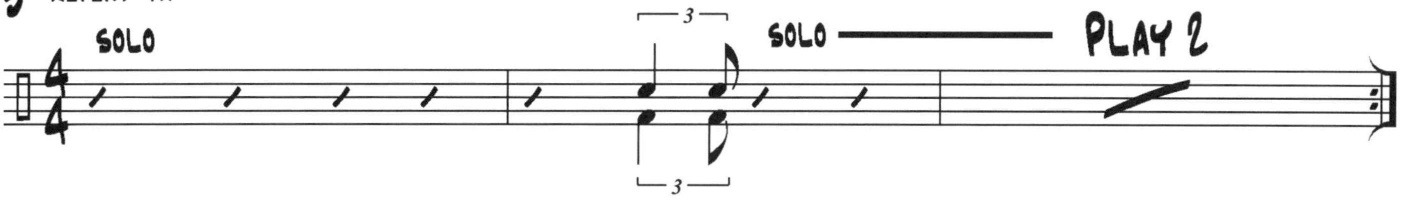

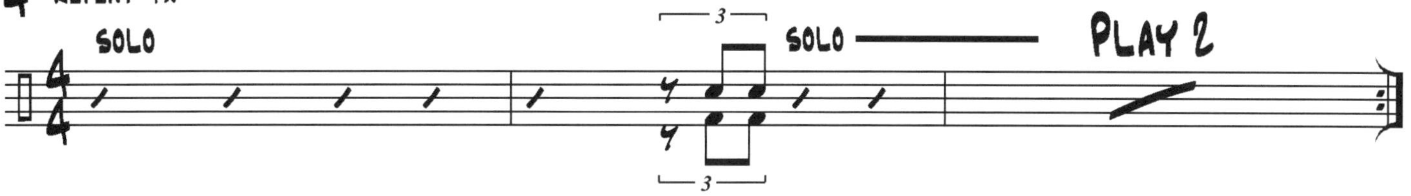

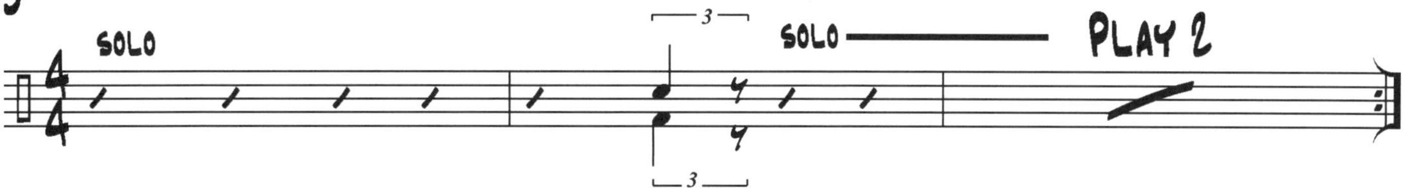

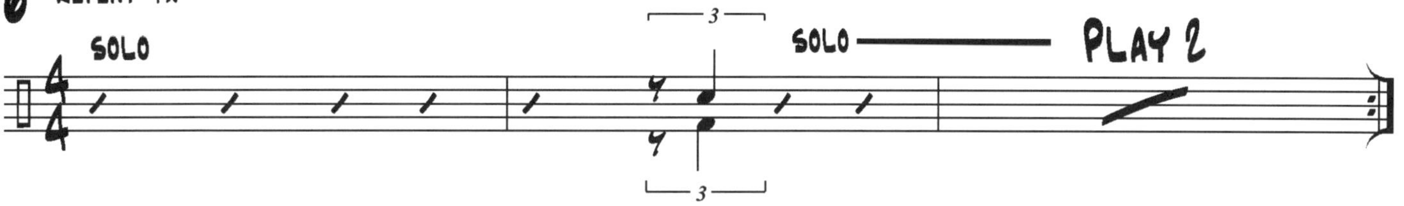

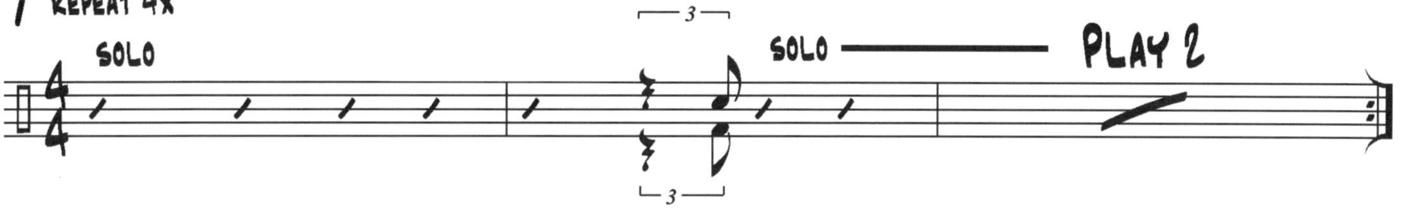

CD Track 35 110 bpm

CD Track 36 132 bpm

7c. Triplet Ensemble Playing 2:

Triplet Element Ensemble Hits on Beat 3

1 Repeat 4x (2 Bars Click up Front)

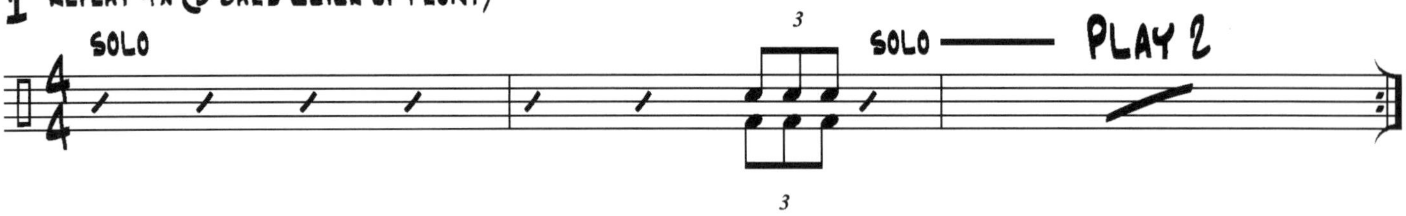

2 Repeat 4x

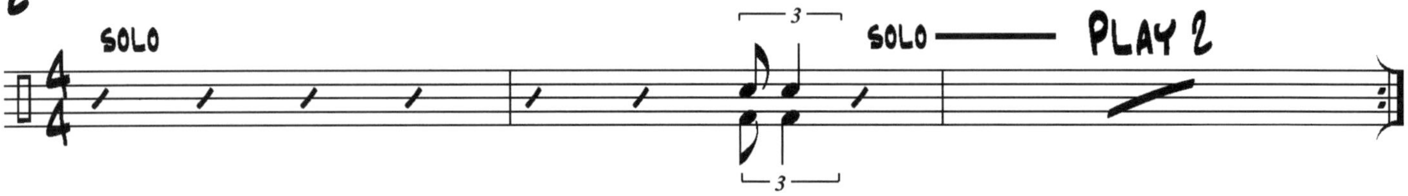

3 Repeat 4x

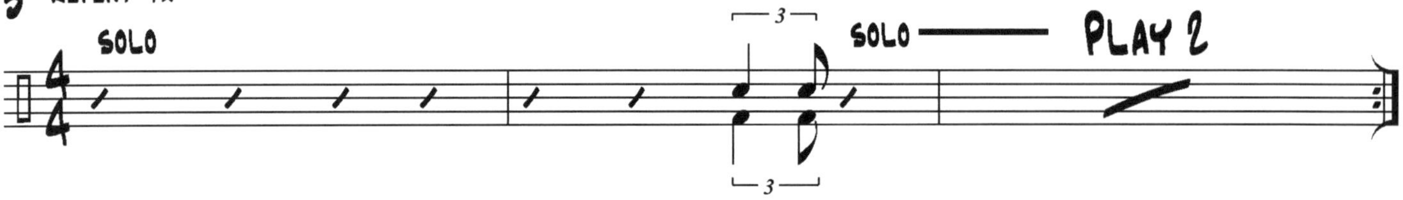

4 Repeat 4x

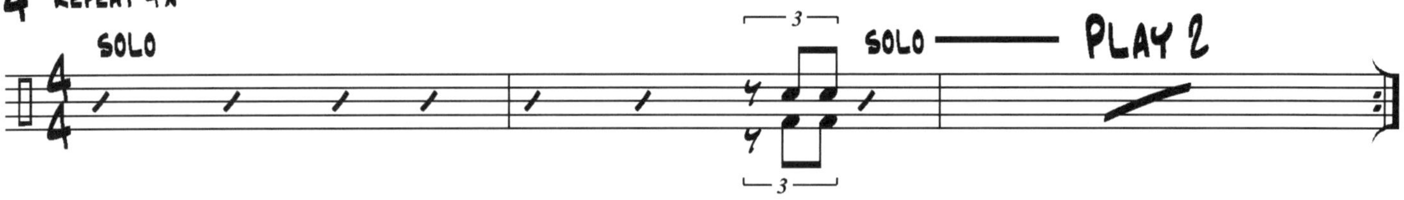

5 Repeat 4x

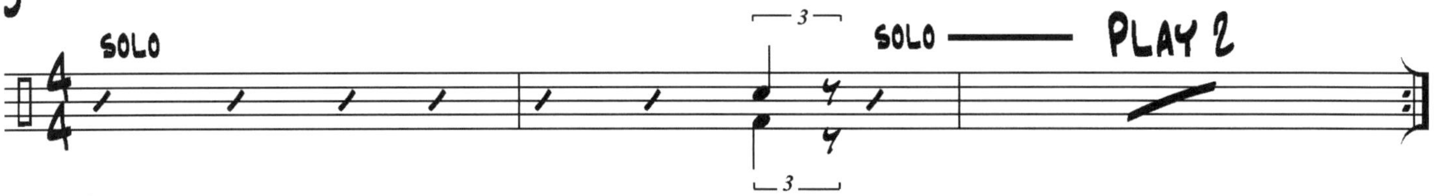

6 Repeat 4x

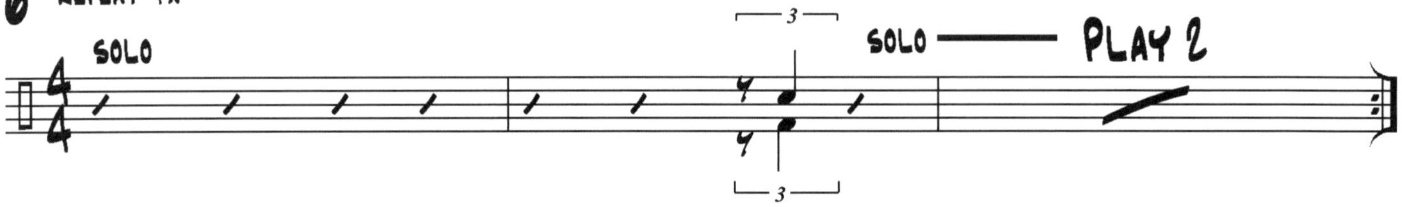

7 Repeat 4x

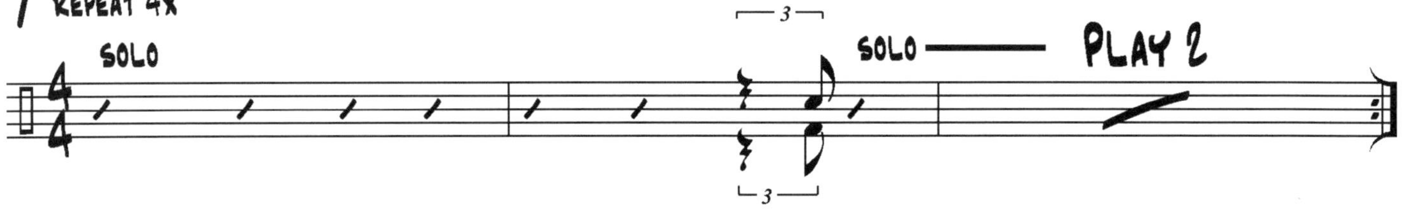

CD Track 37 110 bpm

CD Track 38 132 bpm

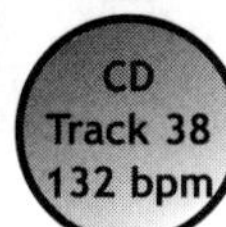

7d. Triplet Ensemble Playing 2:

Triplet Element Ensemble Hits on Beat 4

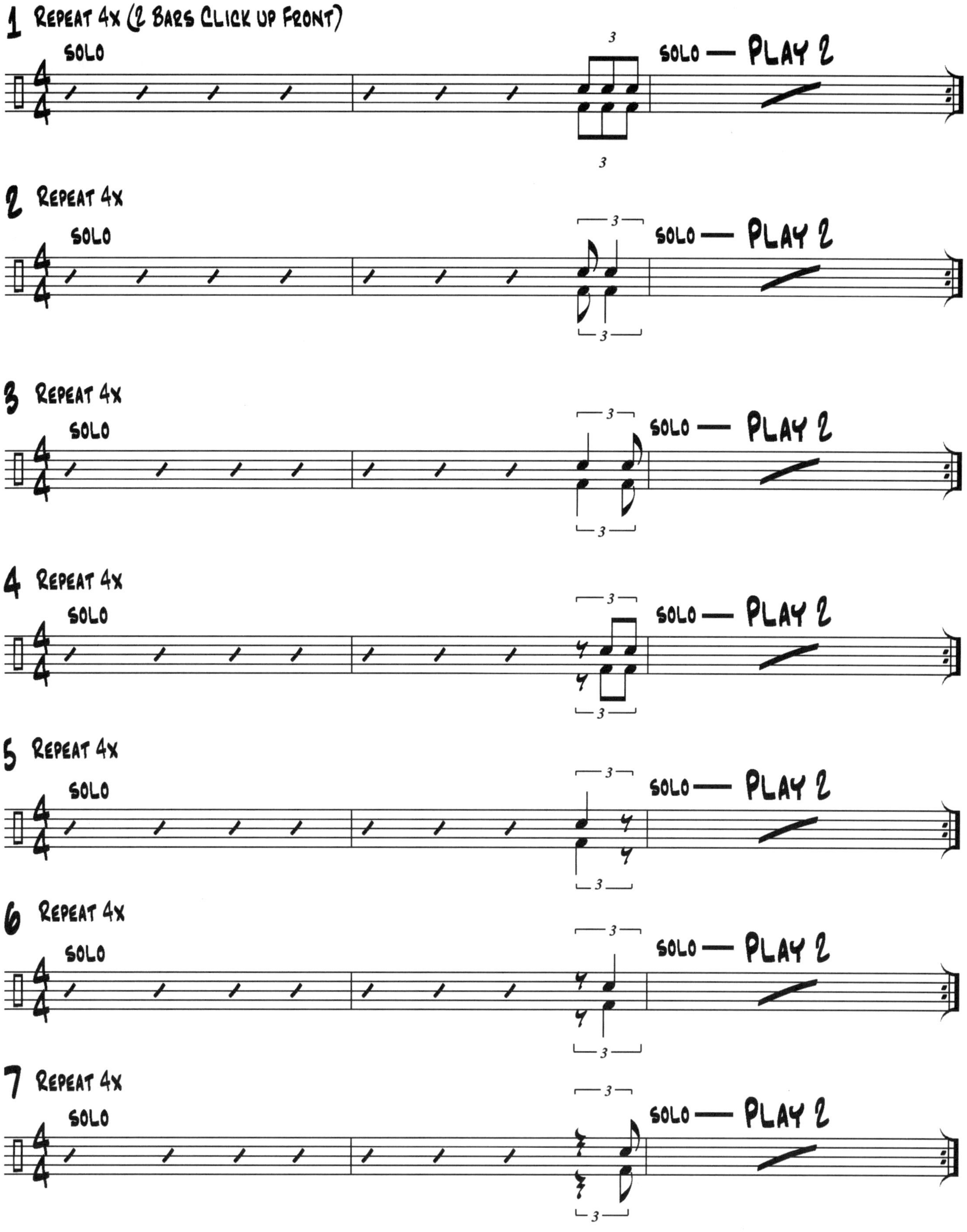
1 Repeat 4x (2 Bars Click up Front)
SOLO
SOLO — PLAY 2
2 Repeat 4x
SOLO
SOLO — PLAY 2
3 Repeat 4x
SOLO
SOLO — PLAY 2
4 Repeat 4x
SOLO
SOLO — PLAY 2
5 Repeat 4x
SOLO
SOLO — PLAY 2
6 Repeat 4x
SOLO
SOLO — PLAY 2
7 Repeat 4x
SOLO
SOLO — PLAY 2

PART 4:
TRIPLET ELEMENT GROOVE OSTINATOS

"Anything worth doing in this world is incredibly difficult to do."
- Jon Forman

"There are no excuses. It is up to you to make things happen."
- John Favicchia

1. Triplet Elements on the Bass Drum

In the groove ostinatos section, you will be using the Elements to improve coordination. With this first set of groove ostinatos, we will be working on bass drum independence. The exercises below show a basic rock groove with all the triplet Elements played for one measure on the bass drum. Start slow, and use a metronome.

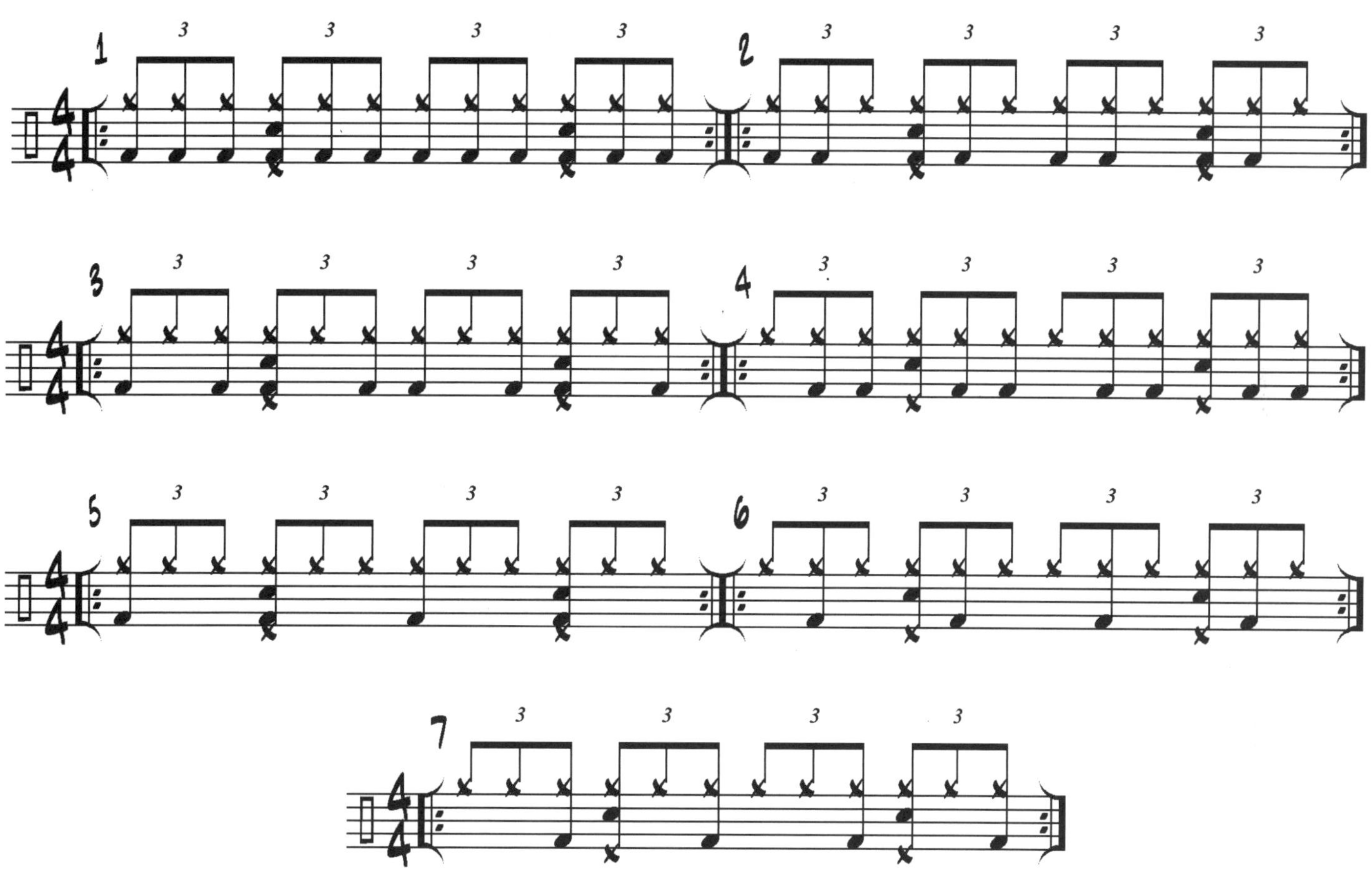

2. Triplet Element Groove Ostinatos

Use these three-limb groove ostinatos in conjunction with the rhythms on pages 84-85 and follow the directions for which limb reads the rhythms.

Bass Drum Reads Variations

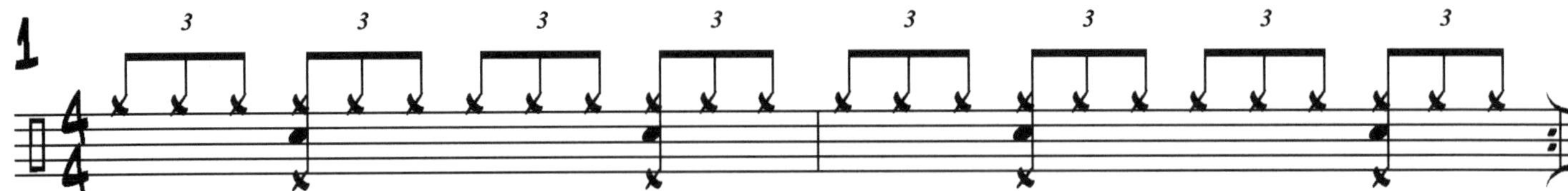

Bass Drum Reads Variations

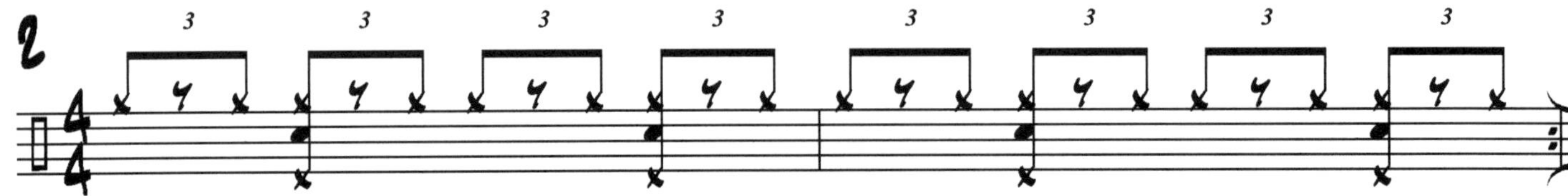

Bass Drum Reads Variations

Snare Drum Reads Variations

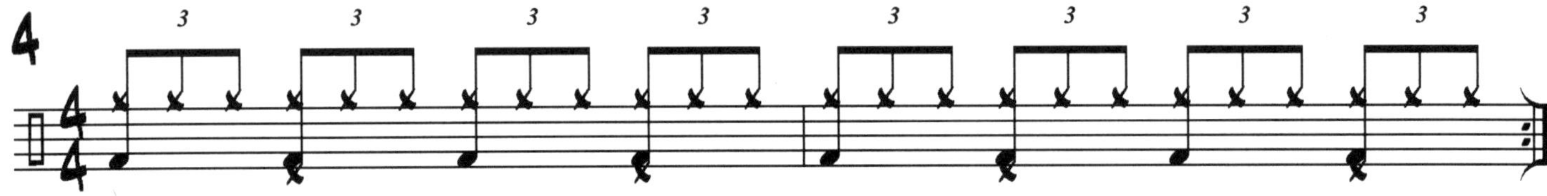

Snare Drum Reads Variations

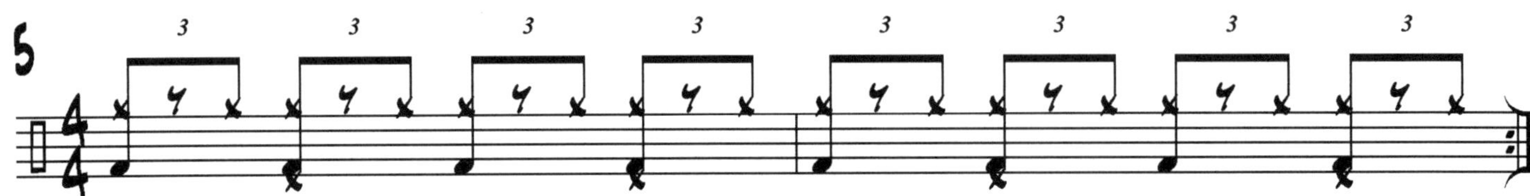

Snare Drum Reads Variations

3. Advanced Triplet Element Groove Ostinatos

Snare Drum Reads Variations

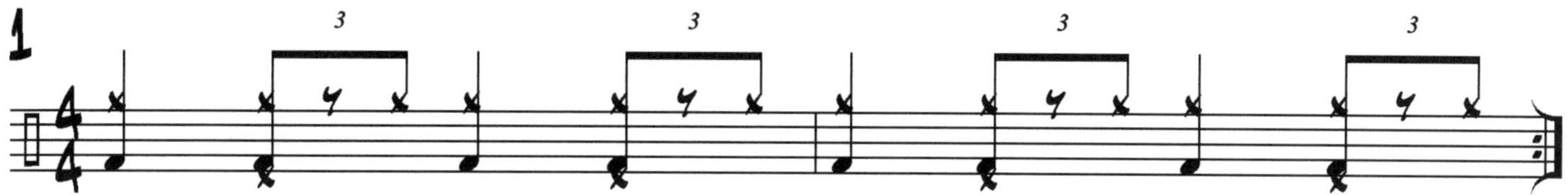

Bass Drum Reads Variations

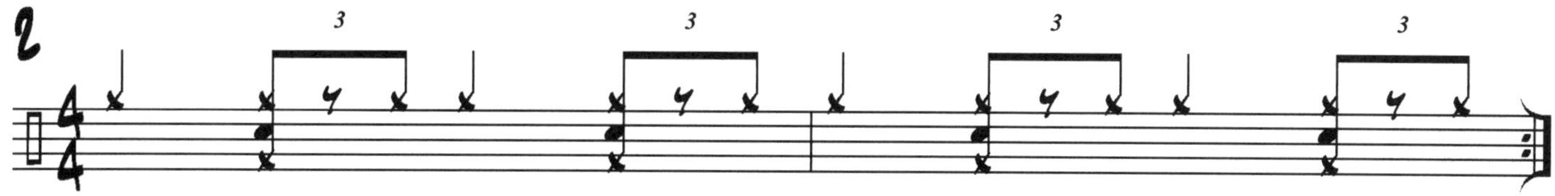

Bass Drum Reads Variations

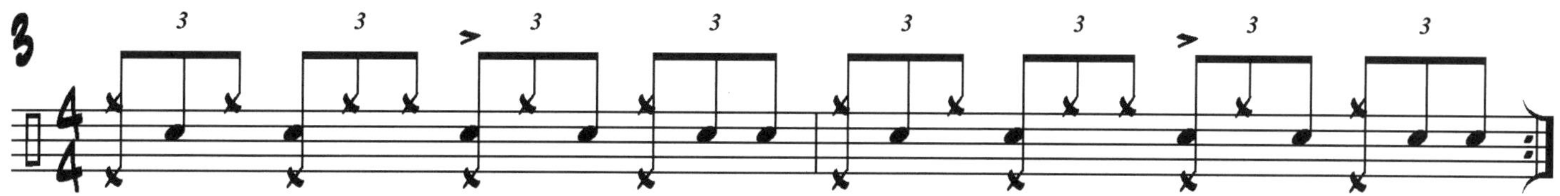

Bass Drum Reads Variations

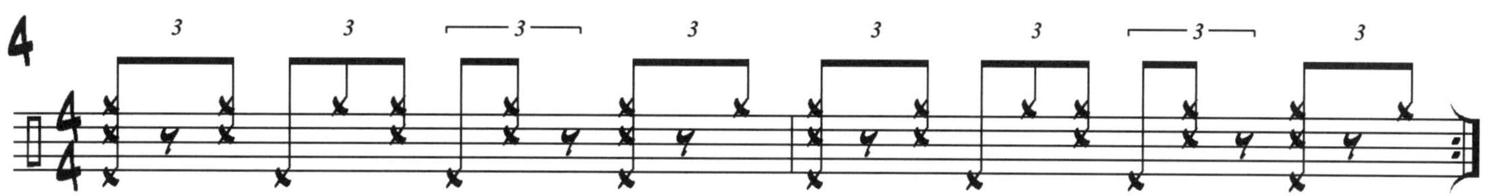

Snare Drum Reads Variations

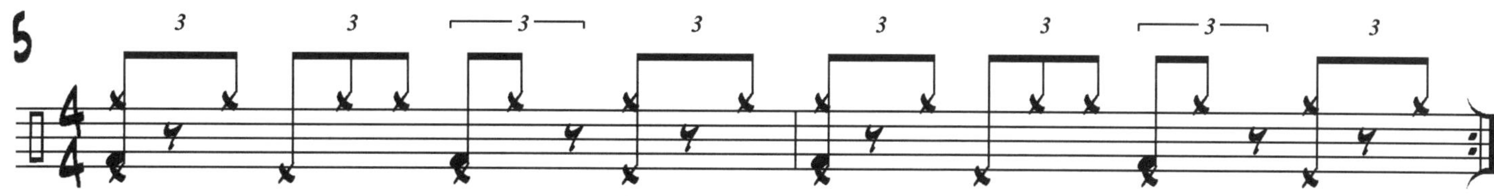

Snare Drum Reads Variations

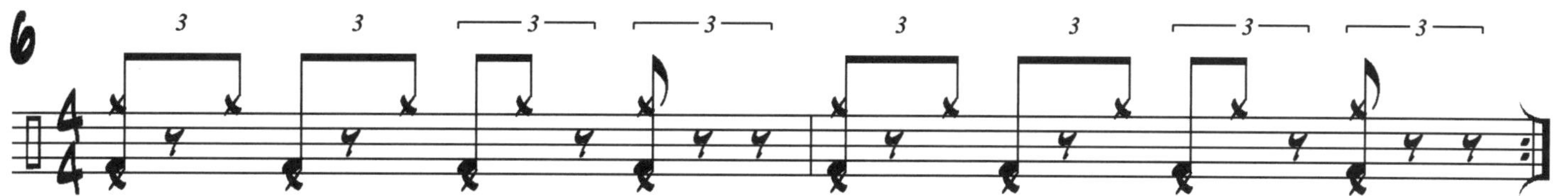

Reading Variations for Sections 2 and 3

These rhythms are to be played with the groove ostinatos presented in parts 2 and 3.

Reading Variations for Sections 2 and 3

These rhythms are to be played with the groove ostinatos presented in parts 2 and 3.

PART 5:
BASS PLAY-ALONGS

"All true artists, whether they know it or not, create from a place of no-mind, from inner stillness."
- James McNeill Whistler

This chapter presents bass play-along loops in various styles for you to practice the Elements.

Rock

CD Track 39

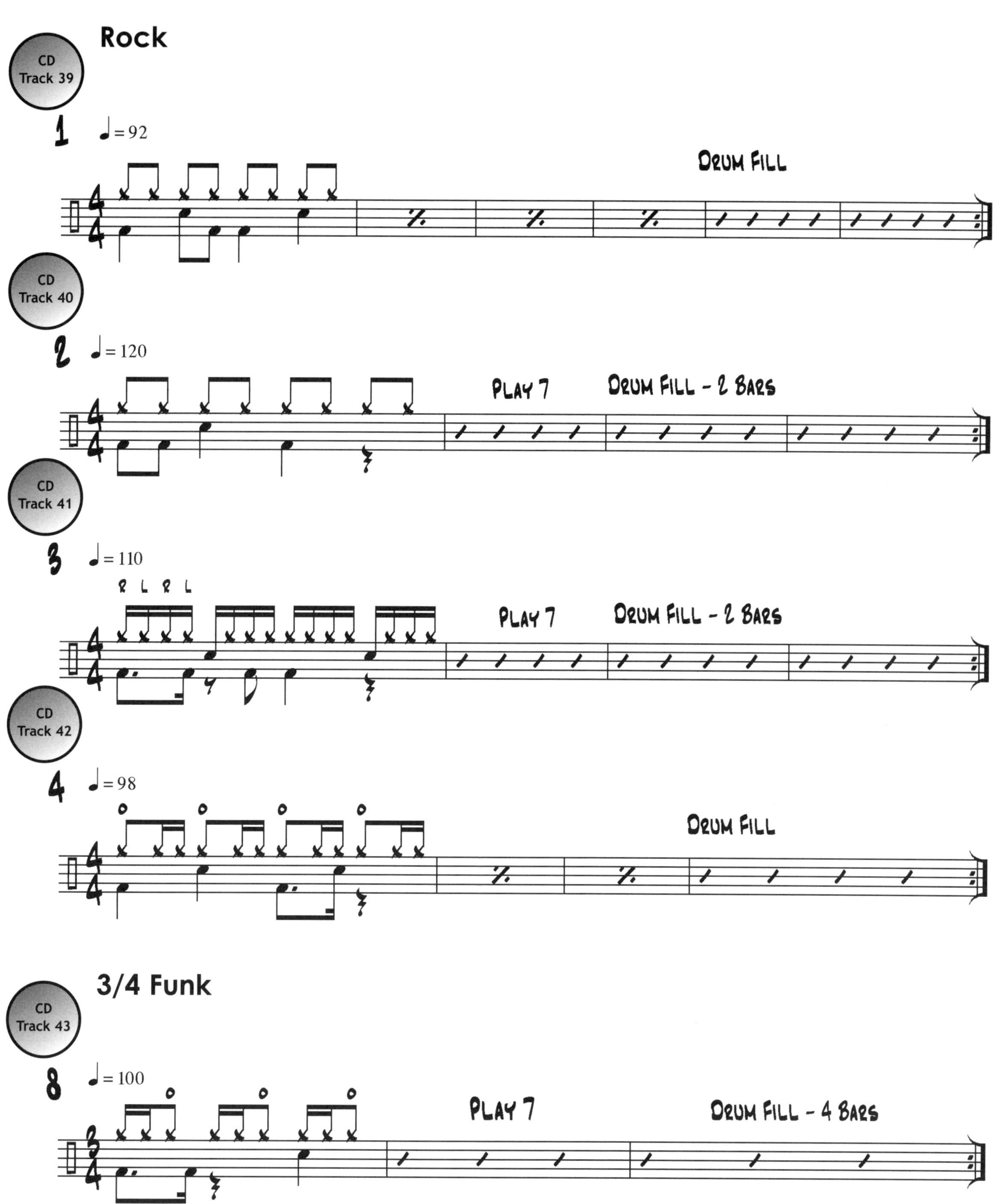

CD Track 40

CD Track 41

CD Track 42

3/4 Funk

CD Track 43

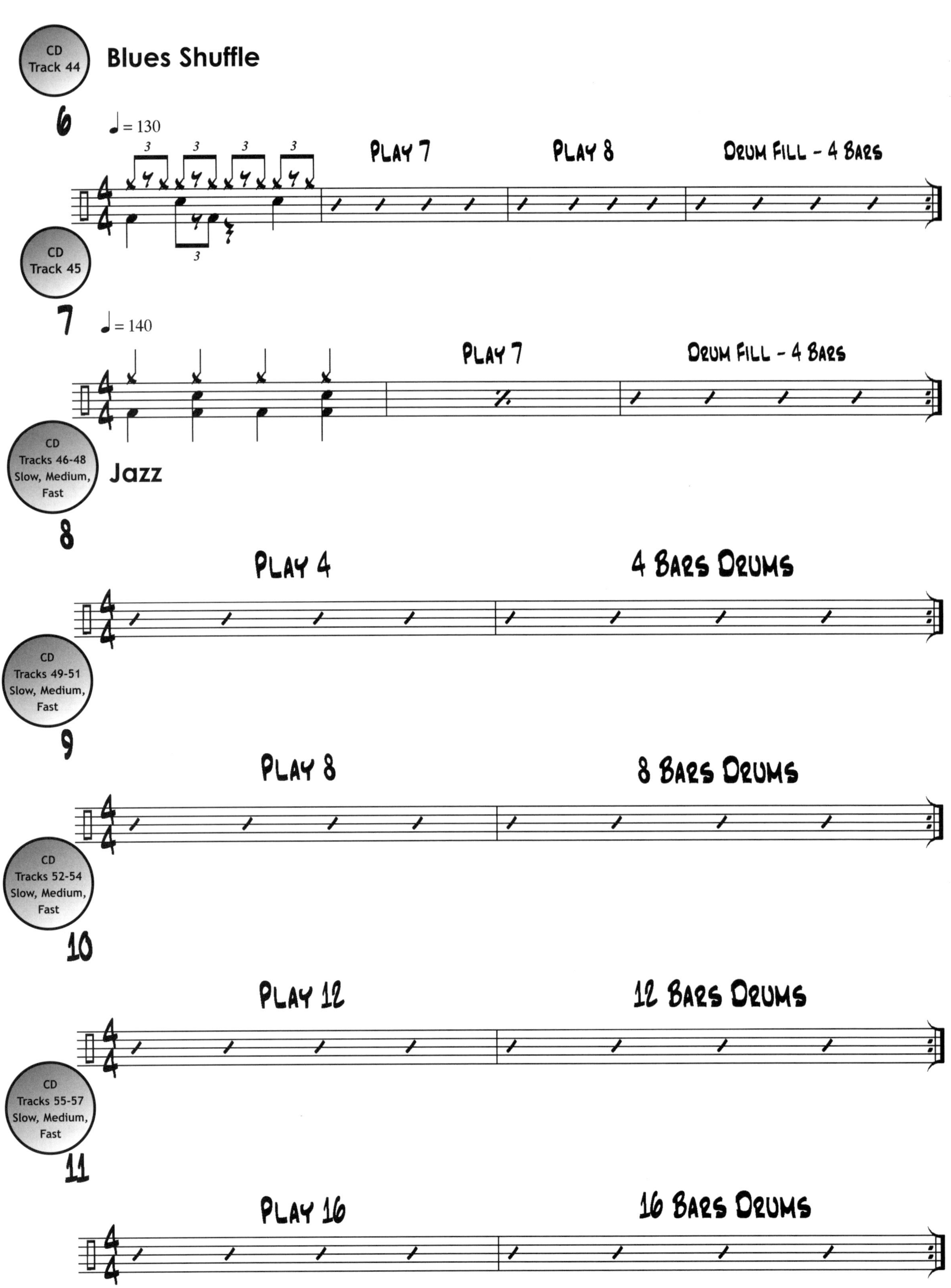

CD Track 44
Blues Shuffle
6
♩ = 130
PLAY 7
PLAY 8
DRUM FILL - 4 BARS
CD Track 45
7
♩ = 140
PLAY 7
DRUM FILL - 4 BARS
CD Tracks 46-48
Slow, Medium, Fast
Jazz
8
PLAY 4
4 BARS DRUMS
CD Tracks 49-51
Slow, Medium, Fast
9
PLAY 8
8 BARS DRUMS
CD Tracks 52-54
Slow, Medium, Fast
10
PLAY 12
12 BARS DRUMS
CD Tracks 55-57
Slow, Medium, Fast
11
PLAY 16
16 BARS DRUMS

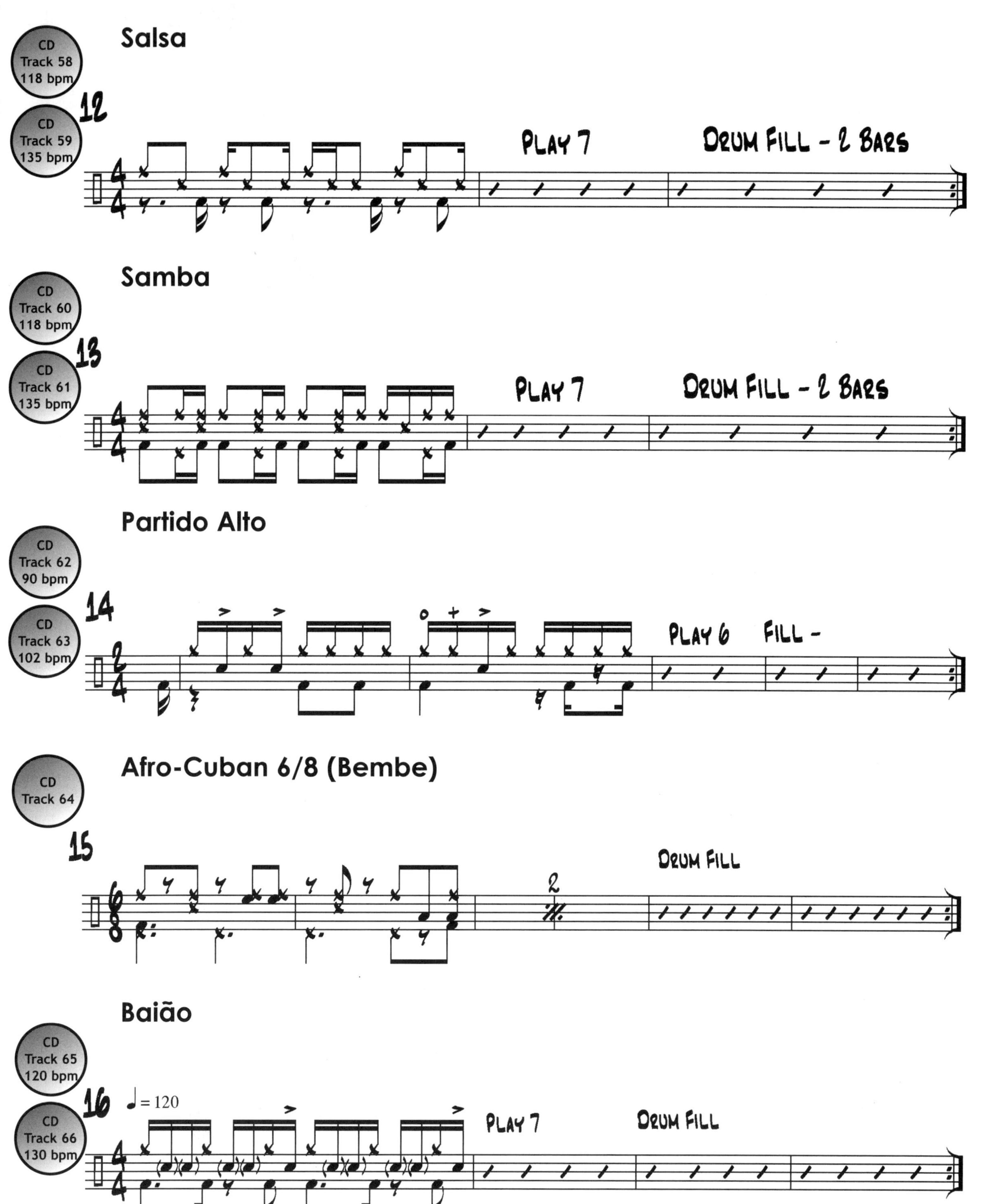
K Ca Sc Ti V Cr Mn Fe Co Ni Cu Kr
Salsa
CD Track 58 118 bpm
CD Track 59 135 bpm
12
PLAY 7
DRUM FILL - 2 BARS
Samba
CD Track 60 118 bpm
CD Track 61 135 bpm
13
PLAY 7
DRUM FILL - 2 BARS
Partido Alto
CD Track 62 90 bpm
CD Track 63 102 bpm
14
PLAY 6
FILL -
Afro-Cuban 6/8 (Bembe)
CD Track 64
15
DRUM FILL
Baião
CD Track 65 120 bpm
CD Track 66 130 bpm
16
= 120
PLAY 7
DRUM FILL

PART 6:
PLAY-ALONG CHARTS

"Funk It Up"

On this track, I recommend three things: groove, groove, and groove! Make up your own rock/funk groove and follow the chart. On the turnaround stop right before the second A section, you can play a fill or leave space. It's up to you. Try playing a fill using the Elements before the keyboard solo; this is a good space for you to practice playing short fills. Keep your ears open and make sure to lock the bass drum with the bass player—on this type of song, the bass drum/bass guitar lock is crucial. Keep grooving and enjoy.

"From Silence to Sound"

This is one of my favorite tracks to play—it has it all: great groove playing as well as plenty of room to solo.

I approach this song in a compositional manner. I like the groove to start out sparse and then build constantly into the drum solo. Once the drum solo breakdown occurs, I then start the build all over again, but this time using improvised Elements. For example, at the beginning of the solo, try using the Elements random voicing exercise. Choose an Element or two and then randomly choose a part of the drum set on which to play it. This will give the opening section of your solo a very spacious feel, and a simple but tasty beginning to expand on! Then slowly build the solo to the end, finishing with all you've got!

CD Track 69

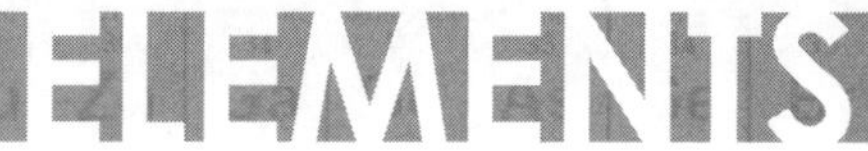

"Rock It Out"

This track has a contemporary rock feel. Laying down a big strong groove is the key. Be sure to listen to the bass line and lock your kick drum with it. Following the song form should dictate to you when to play hi-hat and when to go to the ride. I play the hi-hat on the A sections and the ride on the B sections. Feel free to open up and play some fills as the songs builds toward the end. Stay in the pocket and have fun!

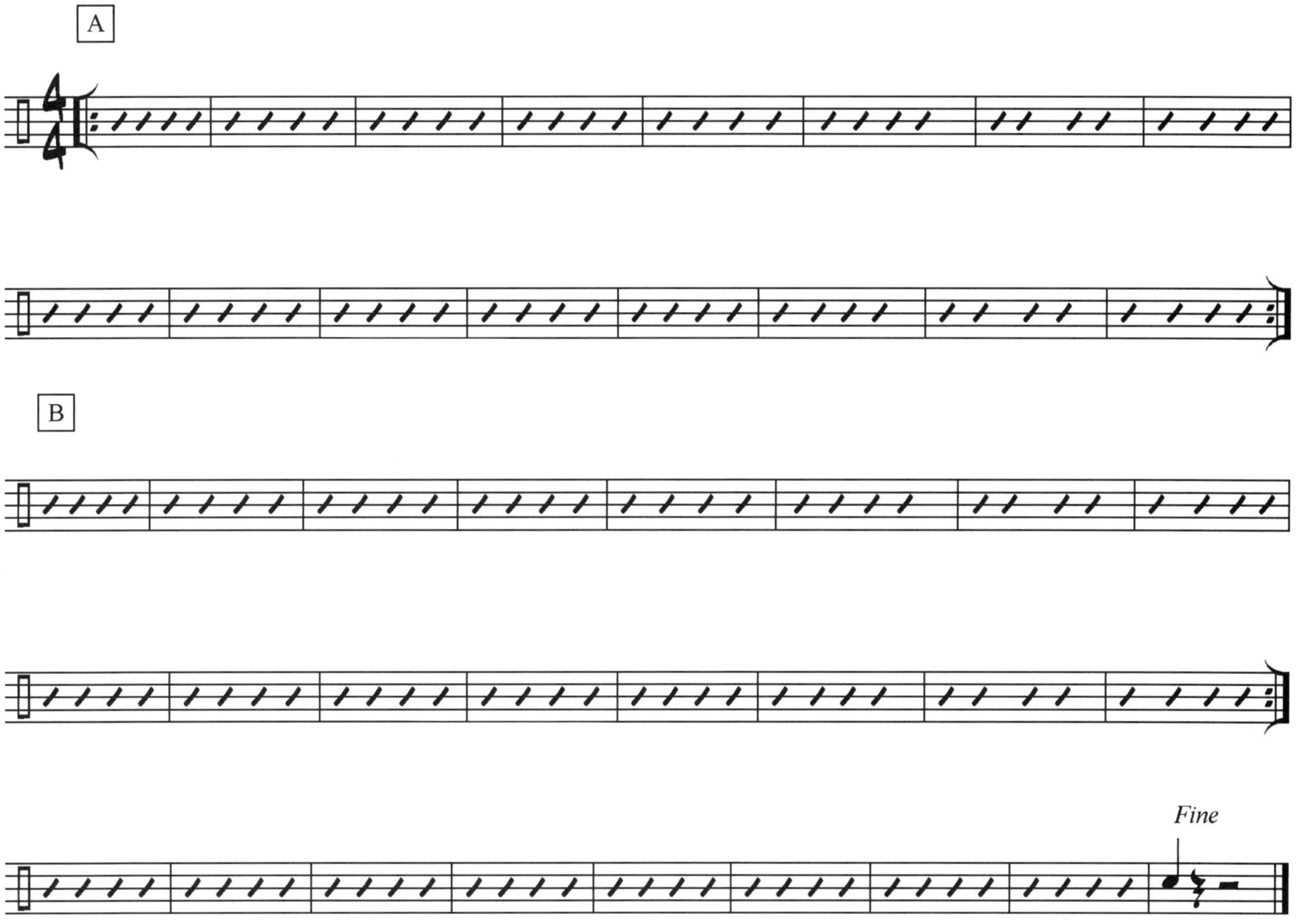

"Coincidence"

This tune has a fusion/funk feel and is in 3/4. The hi-hat plays on the upbeats.

Session Notes

Keep the intro simple, with no backbeat.

A Section: Notice that I play the 16th notes on both my x-hat and main hi-hats. This helped to give the groove a looser feel as well as add a lot of dynamics.

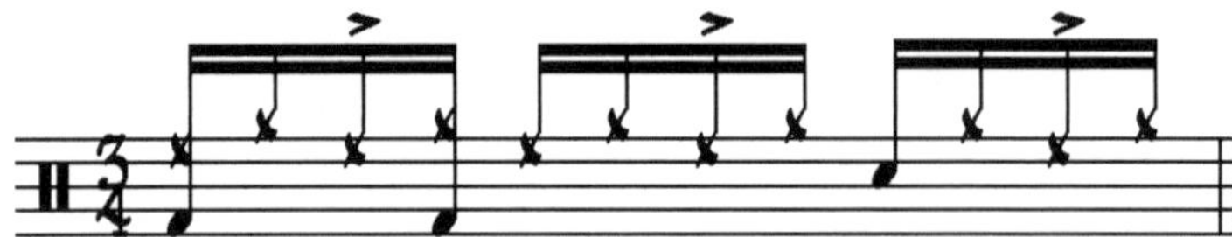

B Section: I played a mixed sticking groove broken up between the ride and snare drum. I also moved my left hand over to the hi-hat sometimes instead of the snare.

E Section: Play a simple groove to set up the drum solo at F.

F section: The drum solo is only 24 bars long, so I tried to come out strong right from the start. Keep in mind you are playing over a keyboard and bass vamp, so that should help determine what you play in the solo.

G Section: Try playing the groove from the B-section for the first few bars and then start to open up and create some excitement.

Focus Points:

Bar 31: This bar has the main ensemble hits. Go over these individually and try to get comfortable with filling around the hits.

Drum Solo: Play the drum solo over a few times to get used to playing over the vamp.

CD Track 70 w/ Drums

CD Track 71 w/o Drums

"Coincidence" Chart

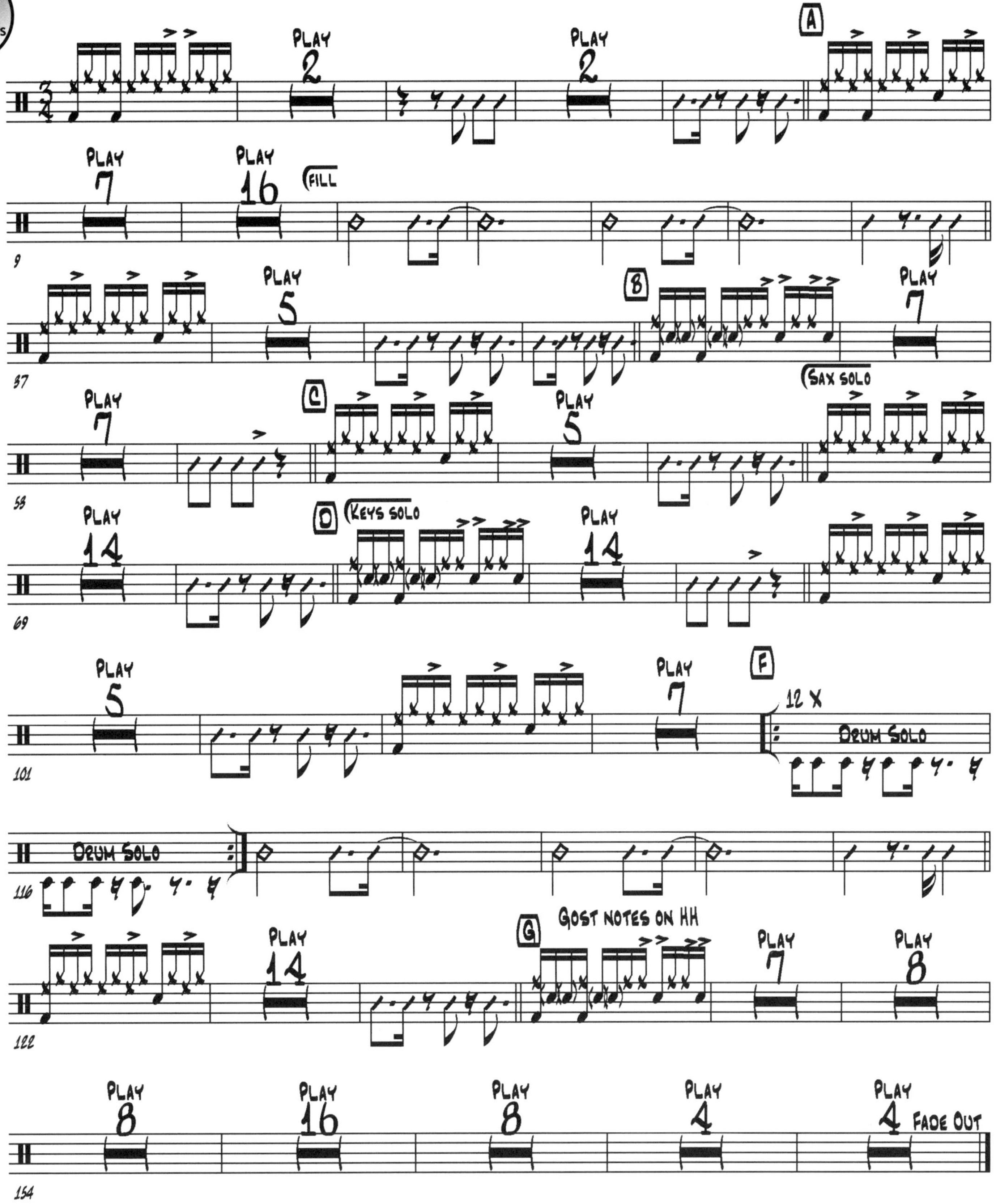

"Te Estremeces"

This tune has a Latin jazz feel. It is in 3-2 clave and written in cut time.

Session Notes

In my opinion this song calls for a laid-back Latin jazz feel. The tune originally had vocals where the guitar melody is, so when I first heard the track my instinct was to play as simple as possible so the melody stood out. I play the same groove throughout the entire tune.

A Section: I play the groove on the hi-hat.

B Section: I move the groove to the ride cymbal.

Other than that, all I was thinking about was to interact with the soloist and create some excitement as well as catch some of the unison lines that the band played.

Focus Points:

D Section: This is a rather syncopated ensemble section. I recommend working on this by itself before going through the tune.

Also check out the ending. This line can be a bit tricky as well.

CD Track 72 w/ Drums

CD Track 73 w/o Drums

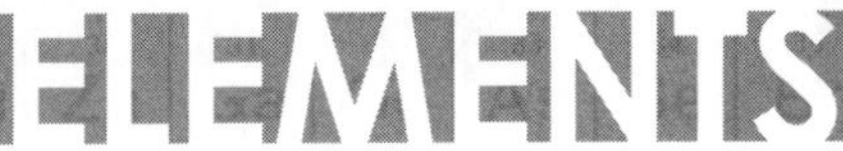

"Te Estremeces" Chart

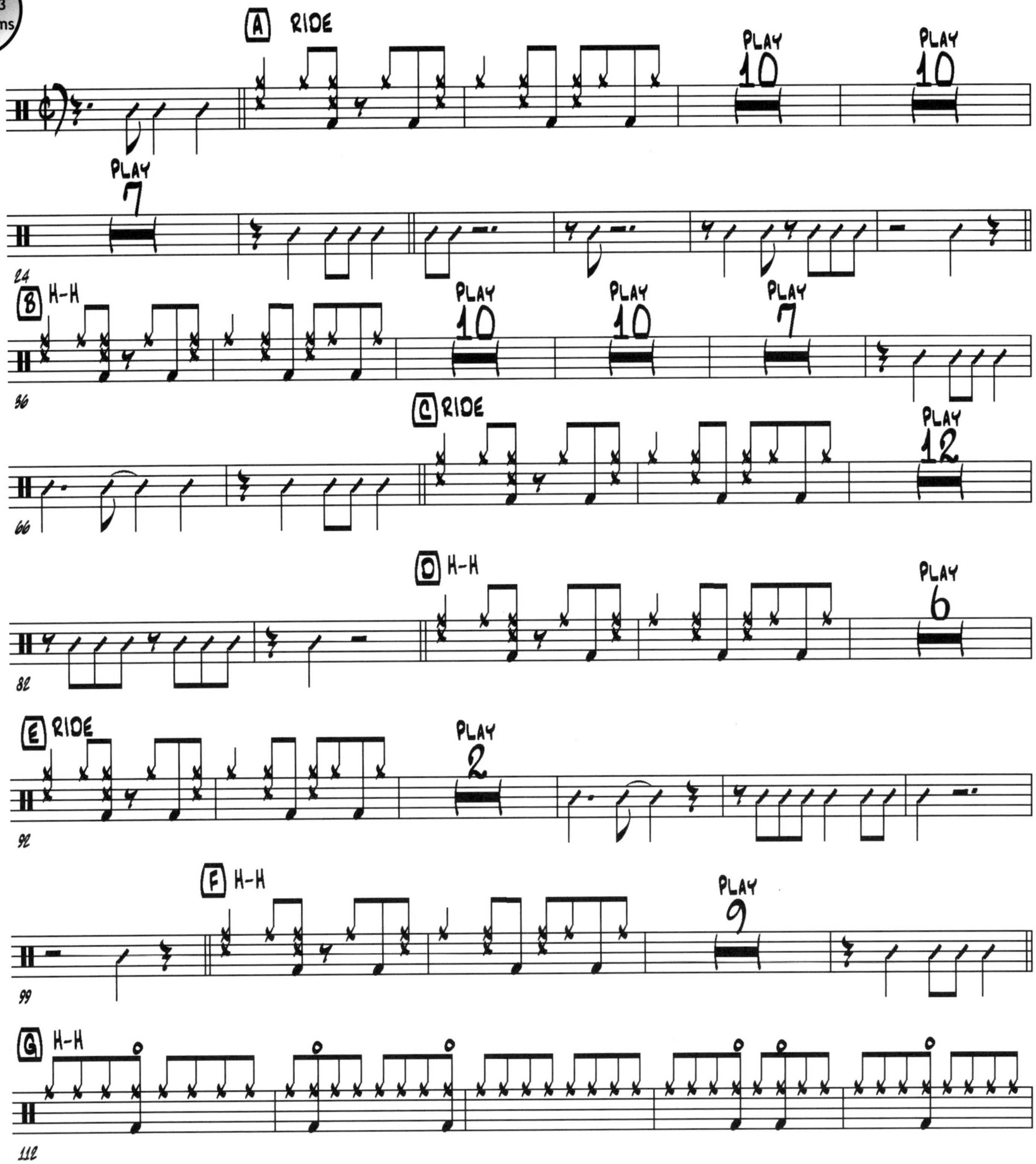

H-H
117
122
SONGO (BONGO BELL)
PLAY 8
PLAY 6
(FILL
PLAY 16
127
PLAY 16
PLAY 16
PLAY 16
PLAY 16
PLAY 16
PLAY 16
160
PLAY 16
PLAY 16
PLAY 16
PLAY 8
PLAY 7
RIDE
256
PLAY 16
PLAY 7
PLAY 2
320
348

"Animation"

This tune has a rock/funk feel to it.

Session Notes

On this tune I tried to play as little as possible and focus in on the groove. I really wanted to make the guitar stand out on the recording as well as just lay down a solid roove throughout the song. Check out the funk groove in the C section:

Try mixing up the stickings and making it as funky as you can.

Focus Points:

A Section groove:

B Section groove:

C Section groove:

CD Track 74 w/ Drums

CD Track 75 w/o Drums

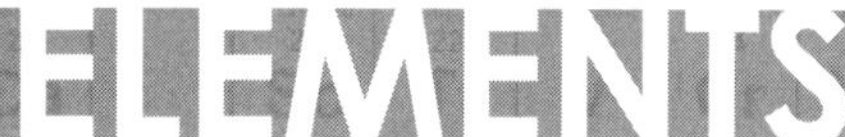

"Animation" Chart

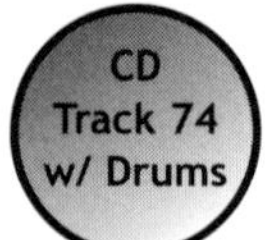

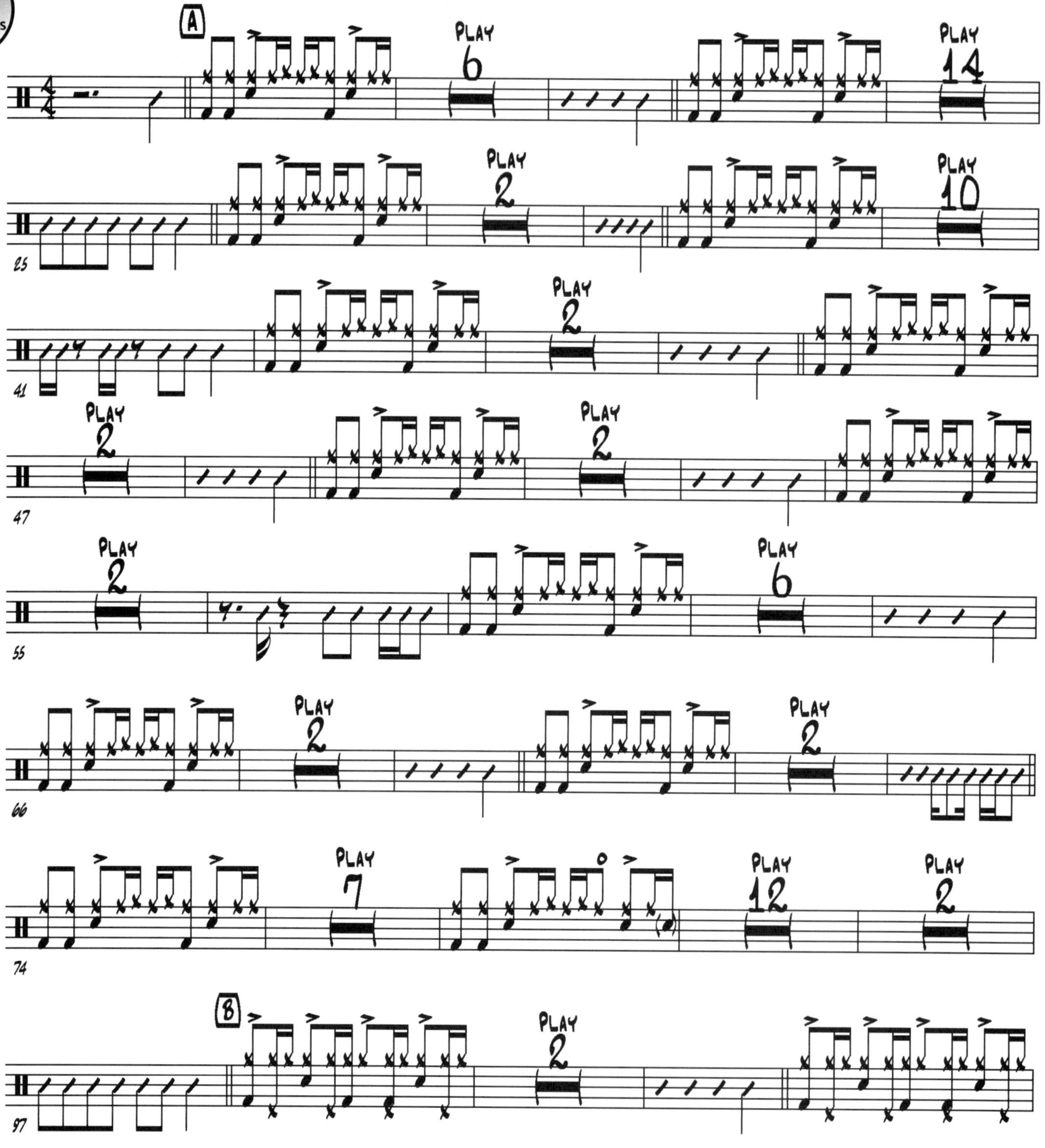

K Ca Sc Ti V Cr Mn Fe Co Ni Cu Kr
PLAY 2
103
PLAY 2
110
PLAY 2
117
PLAY 2
123
PLAY 5
PLAY 6
137
PLAY 10
PLAY 6
151
PLAY 2

"The Gauntlet"

This tune has a fusion feel.

Session Notes

I recommend listening to the track a few times as you follow along with the chart. Keep in mind the unison lines as well as your interpretation of the notes.

Focus Points:

A Section groove:

Bars 32, 35 and 51: Unison lines.

Bar 137: Sax solo groove.

Bars 160 to 174: Drum solo and ensemble hits.

Latin Percussion photo shoot, Garfield, NJ

CD Track 76 w/ Drums

CD Track 77 w/o Drums

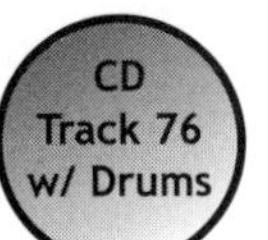

"The Gauntlet" Chart

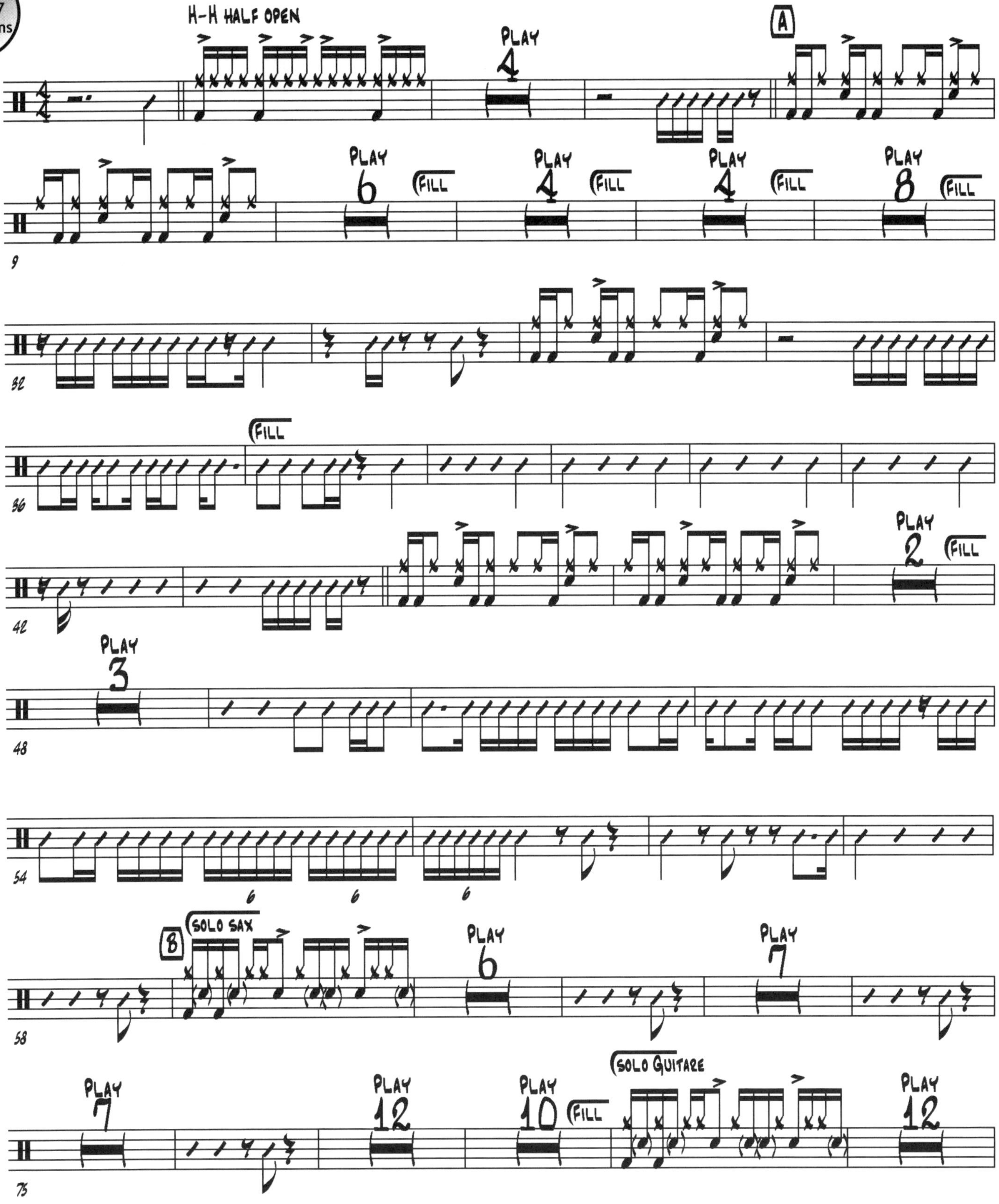

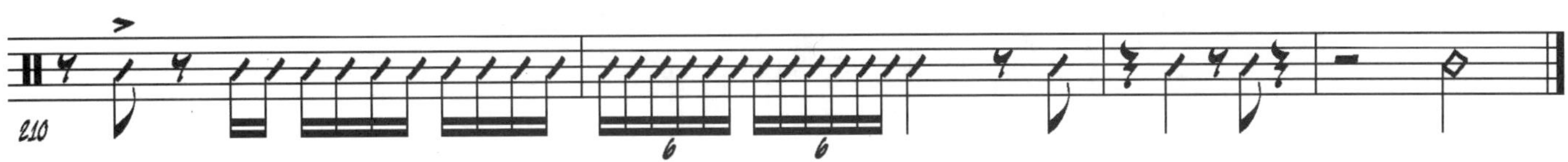

PART 7: TRANSCRIPTIONS

Dom Famularo's ABCs:
A. Always show motion.
B. Be enthusiastic! Energy is inspiring; it is life. And directed positive and focused, it is powerful! Enthusiasm is very important in my life—in every conversation. People react to energy; they feed off of it. Enthusiasm is not draining. It is empowering !
C. Carpe Diem: Life is in the moment—NOW!

- Dom Famularo

Introduction Solo

Here you will find transcriptions of some of my solos from my *Dharma* CD. These are real-world examples of how the Elements work to help create musical and exciting solos. Notice where the highlighted sections are, these are the sections of the solos where I was totally in the zone thinking of the Elements!

Remember, this is a transcription of what I played in the moment. The routines presented in the earlier sections of this book are what gave me the vocabulary to improvise this way.

In this section of the book, the gray bands behind the accents illustrate the places where I have utilized the Elements in the solo.

CD Track 79

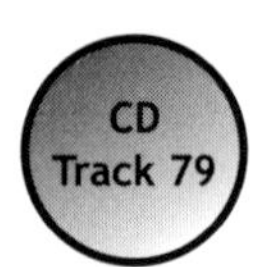

"The Gauntlet" Solo

Again, here the gray boxes highlight where I have used the Elements.

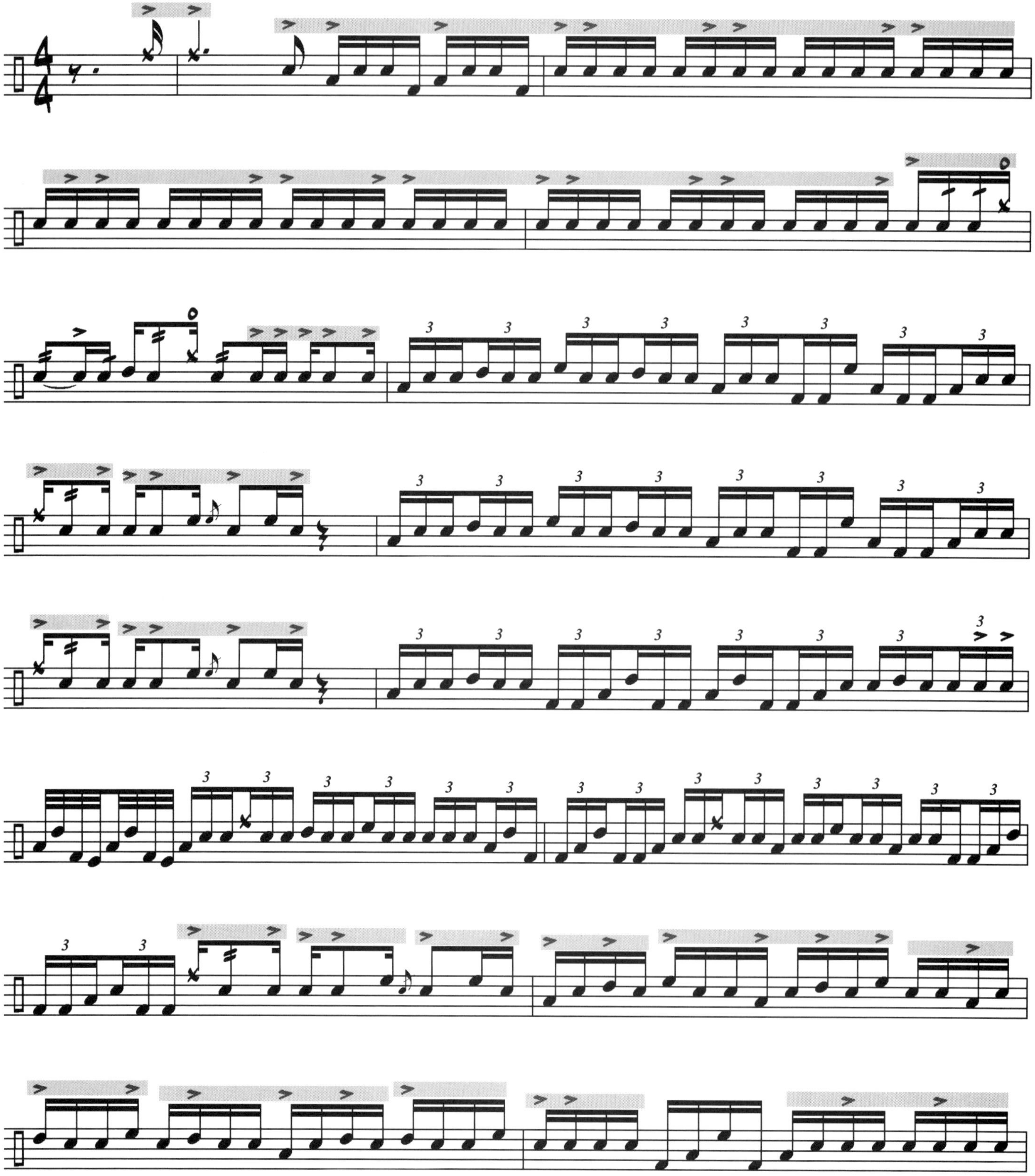

PASIC 2005 (L to R): Simon Miller, Dom Famularo, Steve Gadd, Neil Garthly,
Ryan Carver, John Favicchia, Brian VerStraten.

"World Time II" Solo

ELEMENTS

"Dharma" Solo

CD Track 82

Soloing With Elements 6 & 11

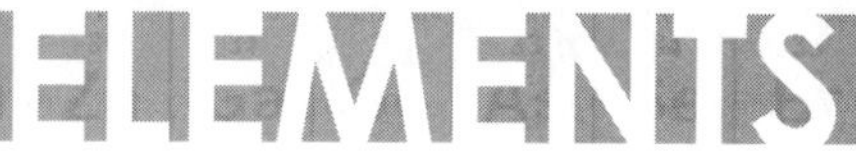

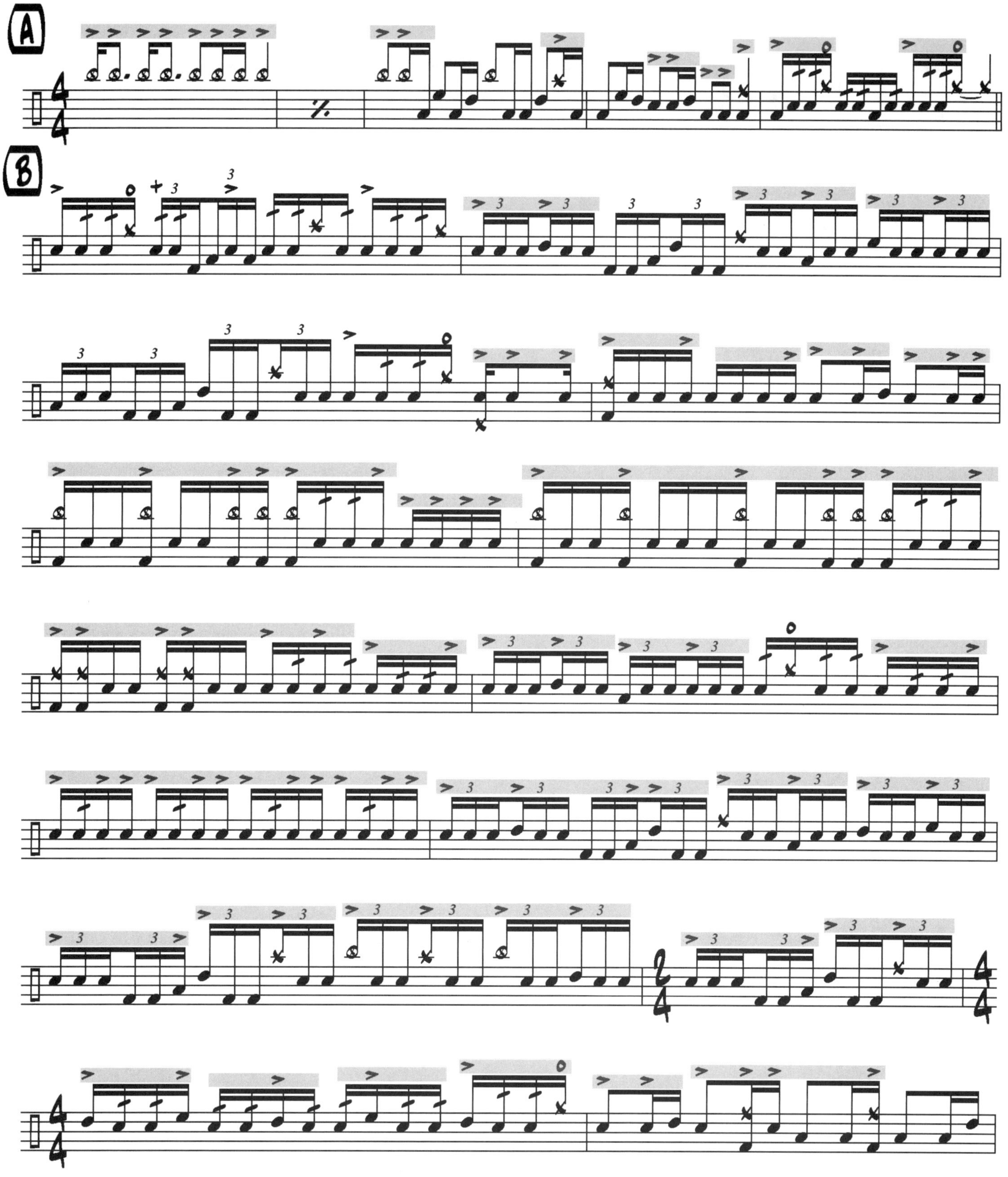

John's Setup

I am a **Yamaha** drummer. There is no way around it for me; I have tried and endorsed other kits but always come back to Yamaha. The sound of their drums is in my head and that's that! I have three kits and love them all. They all have their different uses for me. My Recording Custom kit is my all around kit. I have been lucky enough to have had the opportunity to tour with them many times in Europe. They always have a great sound, whether in a small club or large concert hall.

On my albums, *World Time* and *Dharma,* I used my Maple Custom kit. I feel they give me a very big and warm tom sound, plus the bass drum has a very big sound. I have been keeping them miked up in my studio for all my recording needs.

I recently got 2 Birch Custom Absolute kits. I am using one kit for studio and the other for all my live gigs. I really love them. They have a really nice tone plus a great blend between the toms and bass drum.

I endorse and love **Sabian** cymbals. In February 2005 I was lucky enough to go to the Sabian warehouse and hand-pick my cymbal setup. What an awesome experience. These guys at Sabian are not only great people but they make some *amazing* cymbals. I'm very happy to be part of the Sabian team! If you want to hear my cymbals, check out my profile on sabian.com. You can hear all the cymbals they make—not just the ones I am using. This is a great way to find out what Sabian cymbals are right for you.

I endorse **Vic Firth** drumsticks. I use the SD9, SD10, and 5B Models, depending on the gig. They are great-feeling sticks. The SD9 Driver has an acorn-type tip that makes the ride cymbal sound great while the 5B has a thicker shank for a more meaty sound and feel. I also use Dom's Pads Sticksfor warm-up and practice.

I endorse **Remo** drumheads. They are very consistent and have great sound and feel. I use different models depending on the musical situation, but generally I use clear Ambassadors on the tops and bottoms of my toms, a coated Ambassador on the snare, and a PowerStroke 3 on the bass drum.

I have been playing **Latin Percussion** for as long as I can remember, and it's great to now be one of their endorsers. I love the tone and feel of all their bells, and they help me express myself in all the styles of music I play. I recently added the Compact Congas and Bongos to my kit: Awesome stuff!

I recently started to use and now endorse **Hansenfutz** practice pedals. They are fantastic for practicing foot technique.

As far as practice pads go, I endorse **HQ Percussion** Real Feel Practice Pads. I have been using them for as long as I can remember. Simply the best.

I also endorse **Samson** microphones. I use the Drum 8 pack at all my clinics.

In the studio and for my live drum clinics I use **Super Phones** high-end studio headphones. They are the best! The isolation allows me to hear exactly what my drums sound like on tape while I am recording, as well as get a great monitor mix for my drum clinics.

I also endorse the *Turn It Up & Lay It Down* play-along series of CDs by DrumFun. At this point there are 6 volumes in many styles. I play to some tracks at my clinics as well as have my students go through them! Recently Hudson Music published a series of companion books to some of the CDs. Check them out.

Recently I was turned onto the **Beatnik Rhythmic Analyzer**. This is an amazing tool to gauge how accurate your time is. I have been part of the Beatnik team for a while now, and I must say it is a great product and great team of guys to work with.

I endorse **Axis** pedals. I had been looking for a lighter and faster pedal for some time. When I was at my friend Derek Roddy's studio, I noticed how great these pedals felt. I had to get one! Thanks to Derek for hooking me up with Axis. Great pedals!

I have played **Factory Metal Percussion** for a while now and have made some really interesting and unique sounds with their instruments.

John's Setup (cont.)

John's Drums:
YAMAHA BIRCH CUSTOM ABSOLUTE NOUVEAU SERIES
(Remo drumheads and Yamaha hardware)
- 10x8 Tom
- 12x8 Tom
- 14x14 Floor Tom
- 16x16 Floor Tom
- 13x5.5 Brass Snare
- 22x18 Bass Drum
- Sub Kick

LP PERCUSSION
- Drumset Timbale
- Conga Compacts
- Bongo Cowbell
- Salsa Cowbell
- 1 Cha-Cha Cowbell wi/Gajate Bracket for foot pedal

SABIAN CYMBALS
- HHX Evolution Ride 20"
- HHX Groove Hats 14"
- HHX Evolution O-Zone Crash 16"
- HHX Studio Crash 16"
- HHX Evolution Mini-Chinese 14"
- Chopper 10"
- HHX Evolution Splash 12"
- HH China Kang 10"
- HHX Groove Hats 13"
- HHX Xtreme Crash 16"

Acknowledgements

I want to personally thank you for your interest in my *Elements* book. I am very happy to finally be able to share this with everyone. I have toured my Elements concept around the world for the past 6 years, and it has always been met with great enthusiasm from all the drummers who attend my clinics. The best moments for me are when drummers have their "light bulb" moment and truly understand the Elements concept and its potential.

Very special thanks to my family: my wife Leslie, Mom, Dad, Denise and Noam for their love and support all these years.

Special thanks to Dom Famularo and Joe Bergamini for their constant positive energy and friendship. Thanks for believing in *Elements*! Dom, you are such a great teacher, mentor and friend. Joe, you are the best at all you do. Thanks for your friendship as well!

Thanks to Mike Finkelstein and everyone at Alfred Music, Ryan Carver, David Giacone, Derek Roddy, Todd Sucherman, Johnny Rabb, Tony Maggiolino and everyone at Drummers Collective NYC, Chieli Minucci, Jason Rullo, Bruno Farinelli, Chris Lesso, Mike Sorrentino, Neil Garthly, Ed Hansen, Rick Colby, Nick Manzella, John Miceli, Tony Favichia, Joe Erigo, Sandra Sparks, Tom Silvino, Susan Olivieria, Bob Mieslin, David Grand, Steve Kelly, Al Vetere, Mike Pope, Bill Heller, John Scarpulla, Carl Fischer, Jack Knight, Brad Mason, Bill Harris, Misha Tsiganov, Marco Soccoli, Steve Adelson, Dean Brown, Bruce & Gloria Aitken, Jeff Salem, Nick Lazarev, Dr. David Araten, Dr. Gerard Donnelly, Stephane Chamberland, Dennis Ricci and all at Long Island Drum Center, all the staff at Sam Ash Music locations across the USA, Paul Quinn, and Chris Geith.

Thanks to all my teachers: Jim Chapin, Dom Famularo, Al Miller, Joe Bonadio, Joel Rosenblatt, Mark Walker, Joe Ascione, and Bobby Bernish.

Thanks also to John Whittmann and everyone at Yamaha Drums; Ann MacNally, Chris Stankee, and everyone at Sabian Cymbals; Bruce Jacoby, Matt Connors, and the Remo team; Ben Davies, Joe Testa, Neil Larrivee, and everyone at Vic Firth; Mark Wider at Samson/Zoom; Karen and Chuck Blashaw at Axis Pedals; Steve Nigohosian, Angelo Arimborgo, and Memo Acevedo from Latin Percussion; Mark Cubranich at Hansenfutz; Scott Srittmater at Beatnik; and Spencer Strand at DrumFun.

John's CDs

John's *Dharma* & *World Time* CDs are available at www.cdbaby.com and on iTunes.

REVIEWS OF JOHN'S CDs:

DRUM RING INTERNATIONAL:
John Favicchia's new 2001 CD release, *Dharma*, is truly a work of art. Fusion in every sense of the word, Dharma is a melting pot, a potpourri of musical influences from around the world. The CD features some of the best drumming I've heard in a long time. Favicchia has the perfect blend of chops and musicality; never over playing, yet always leaving you wanting more. Dharma is full of poly-rhythmic interplay, mixed meter, rhythmic displacement, slammin' back-beats, dynamic cymbal work, melodic drum solos, and all the energy & technique you'd expect from a world-class drummer. *Dharma* is full of radio-worthy songs that could fit into the commercial radio format, although thankfully Favicchia doesn't seek to tailor his CD to that genre. Favicchia has obviously invested a great deal of his soul in this music. Wait till you hear Favicchia's burnin' drum solo in the middle section of "The Gauntlet!" John simply tears it up baby! The second of Favicchia's self-produced albums, Dharma is a 'must have' for any fusion lovers CD library and is well worth the price of admission.
- Bart Elliott, Drum Ring International

JAZZIZ MAGAZINE
One of the great joys of being an independent self-released artist is not having to constrain a wide variety of interests to fit into anyone's marketing scheme. On a deeply spiritual level, "Dharma" is a Sanskrit word for one's purpose in life, the reason one is put on this earth. For the New York native and popular, well traveled jazz musician, that means hitting the skins with an amazing group of Big Apple musicians at a club or in the studio. Favicchia expands upon the strengths of his first disc, *World Time*: brilliant melodies, wondrous eclecticism and tight ensemble playing-with an even wider variety of stylistic excursions, an exciting array of all-star guests (David Mann, Harvie Swartz, Steve Khan, Dean Brown, Chieli Minucci) and, stronger showcases for his ever evolving skills as a timekeeper (including two drum solo tracks).

CYBER-DRUM REVIEW:
John Favicchia's *World Time* is well-named and gives the listener ample opportunity to appreciate Favicchia's knowledge and abilities within the world of drumming. Favicchia delves into a wide sampling of rhythms and textures: cool contemporary fusion, large fat grooves, and exotic, worldly patterns. He seems equally at home with Latin styles and jazz ballads, creating suitable moods and feels, and displaying chops in a tasteful manner. Favicchia's grooves are nicely enhanced with the strong musicianship surrounding him, and compelling compositions that stand on their own merit. Favicchia never seems to feel anxious or over-zealous in presenting what he can do. His playing feels relaxed, and he takes his time building solos, suggesting he is more interested in creating the appropriate setting than showing off. And he is quite capable of 'showing off', substantiated by many of his intricate fills. The instrumentalists' are exciting, the compositions are attractive. And John Favicchia helps us to appreciate the value of a world view of life.

CONTEMPO:
That sort of electronic concoction helps us better appreciate the playful sort of combustible human interaction on a project like drummer John Favicchia's *World Time* (Fav Records), a roaring indie release which proves that a studio date can easily capture the buoyant craziness of a hot club show. Favicchia and his core trio of Bob Malach (sax), Bob Gallo (guitar) and pianist Brian Charette run amok on peppy tunes which call to mind some of the artsy, jazzy, post-pop work of the Yellowjackets, as well as the hooky Latin jazz fusion sounds of Spyro Gyra. Malach and Gallo trade off lead melodies most of the time, but Favicchia takes control more often than most drummers do on albums bearing their names, allowing himself space for some aggressive, odd metered fills. While his bandmates do the lion's share of the writing, it's a tribute to Favicchia's melodic instincts that his own Latin hurricane Kukuc is every bit as memorable as Cedar Walton's "Black."
-Jonathan Widran

For more information please visit www.johnfavicchia.com.

MAXIMIZE *YOUR* POTENTIAL!

...with great titles from Wizdom Media.

Eighth-Note Rock and Beyond (Book/MP3 Disc) by Glenn Ceglia with Dom Famularo: A complete method for developing basic groove vocabulary on the drumset, contains a clearly organized and systematic approach to learning the basic beats that drive rock, funk, and R&B. Includes MP3 disc with 145 play-along beats.

The Weaker Side (Book) by Dom Famularo and Stephane Chamberland: This book addresses the age-old challenge faced by every drummer: how to get the weaker hand and foot closer in skill and dexterity to the stronger side. Using a comprehensive step-by-step set of rhythms, this 52-page book is designed to be practiced one page per week, giving an intensive one-year training session to strengthen the weaker side.

Open-Handed Playing (Book/CD) by Claus Hessler with Dom Famularo: This groundbreaking book offers a step-by-step approach for drummers of all styles to learn and apply the concept of open-handed playing on the modern drumset. Based on concepts developed by Jim Chapin and Billy Cobham, the book outlines the benefits of non-crossed hands, and provides an approachable method for learning this technique. Includes play-along tracks.

Pedal Control (Book/MP3 & Video Disc) by Dom Famularo and Joe Bergamini: A complete approach to improving your foot technique, control, power, and speed in all styles. Contains tons of photographs and step-by-step explanations of pedal strokes, in addition to exercises. The included MP3 disc contains 200 tracks of examples from the book, plus QuickTime videos that clearly explain and demonstrate the various techniques.